Glorified Un-Expectations

Trusting God for His Unfailing Faith, Hope, and Love

Kerri Gene Daniels

Trinity Press Books
A service of Trinity Web Works, LLC.

Author/Writer: Kerri Gene Daniels
Co-Writer/Chief Editor: Lynn Marino, MBA
Chief Designer/Literary Strategist: Tony Marino, MBA

Published by Trinity Press; a service of Trinity Web Works, LLC. Salem, Oregon.

GLORIFIED UN-EXPECTATIONS

Scripture quotations marked (NLT) are taken from:
The Holy Bible, New Living Translation, copyright © 1996, 2004, 2007
by Tyndale House Foundation.
Used by permission of Tyndale House Publishers, Inc., Carol Stream,
Illinois 60188.
All rights reserved.

No part of this publication may be reproduced, stored in a retrieval system,
or transmitted in any way by any means—electronic, mechanical,
photocopy, recording, or otherwise—without the prior permission of the
copyright holder, except as provided by U.S.A. copyright law. Requests for
permission should be made in writing to Trinity Web Works, LLC., 1050
25th Street SE, #13784, Salem, Oregon, 97301, U.S.A..

ISBN-10: 1717195342
ISBN-13: 978-1717195340

Cover photography, layout, and art design: Tony Marino, MBA

First Unit Multimedia Production Team: Kerri Daniels, Rick Daniels,
Lynn Marino, MBA

Special thanks to our friends at Canon, Adobe, Lowell, ASUS and Trinity
Web Works for fashioning so many useful innovative products and
services,

To the City of Salem, Oregon and Salem Police Department, we honor
you and give God the praise for your sheer beauty, tranquil surroundings,
relaxed atmosphere, superb faire, safe environment, and caring people.

To all people, everywhere, let us continue to give unfailing glory and all the
praise to God the Father, and the Son, and the Holy Spirit, by faith,
through our Lord and our Savior, Christ Jesus. Amen.

GLORIFIED UN-EXPECTATIONS

The glory of God is what is breathing and alive today. Everything that you do, everything that you become, everything in you, belongs to Jesus Christ, and He is the One when Un-Expectations occur, He provides grace as He takes you step by step through the unexpected and leads you with your very own life story.

- Kerri Gene Daniels

In Loving Memory of our daughter, Jaelynn Gene Daniels. Thank you, Jesus for our baby girl who is safely at home with You.

KERRI GENE DANIELS

Dedication

Glorified Un-Expectations is dedicated to my mother, Kathie Cecile Eaton.

My mother has been battling cancer for over 20 years. As I am about to release this book, she has fallen victim again to this nasty illness as the breast cancer has metastasized and begun to spread. Mom and dad are on yet another journey as the chemo continues. Mom is simply grateful for every day and wants to enjoy each one to the fullest. Every new day is another new story to be written, to share, because Jesus is always going before our trials and preparing us by filling us with His Grace and His Mercy.

Christmas is my mom's favorite time of year. Every Christmas my mom and dad include in our gifts some kind of jewelry. This past year, her eye was drawn to a sterling silver bracelet with two words engraved into it. She knew immediately this was the perfect gift, yet something inside her spirit spoke to her and said to just hold off and tuck away these two gifts for another time.

When we received the unexpected, heart-wrenching news of mom's prognosis in February, 2018, mom knew within her spirit that now was the time to present my sister and me with these meaningful gifts. My sister had just returned home from visiting her in the hospital, and as she walked toward me with tears in her eyes, she handed me this unexpected gift wrapped in Christmas paper and said, "Open it."

I opened the box, and inside I saw a quote, "Stay strong, know that you can, believe that you can overcome anything, and remember that you are loved." My sister raised her arm up and smiled as she showed me the identical bracelet that was in her box and it read...STAY STRONG.

If ever there was a time I cried the hardest, I believe this was it. These words describe how my mom continues to rise above and overcome. My mom's faith remains strong. Her hope overcomes, and her love rises above in Jesus. Her message; "Stay strong in Jesus Christ, and know that when we are weak, HE is STRONG! Mom, I thank you for showing us how to find our strength in Jesus Christ. It's not only engraved on our bracelets, it will forever be engraved in our hearts, souls, and minds.

Acknowledgements

First and foremost I want to Thank Jesus Christ, my Lord and Savior for this story, His story; my life. Without Him, there is no purpose.

Rick, you are my husband and soulmate. Your love has blessed my life in so many ways. You have shown me that from the moment we said, "I do," our love story was the start of something beautiful. Life with you has been filled with lots of joy, and yes, sorrow, but nothing compares to the moments when you and I go before our heavenly Father in prayer, united as one and surrender our souls to His will for our lives. We can just be together; Jesus, you, and me. Thank you for your faith, your hope, and your love that lasts forever. I cannot imagine this journey with anyone else. I love you.

Jacob and Elijah: my two wonderful sons. You are both a joy to me and your father and I am so proud that God chose me to be your mom. You continue to bring joy to my life every day. I pray that God will continue to bring blessings to your lives, as you live for Jesus and give Him the honor and glory in everything you do.

Mom and dad; Ron and Kathie Eaton; and Gary and Letha Daniels, I thank you for directing and teaching us the truth and love of Jesus Christ. Because of our deepened relationship with Jesus, our lives are far richer. We owe it all to you.

Sherri: my dear twin sister. Though you may be a few minutes older, I was there when your heart took its first beat. You have been by my side ever since and I thank you for our special bond. I cannot imagine life without my twin. Thank you for being strong when I was weak and taking care of my family when I could not. I will love you forever.

To the rest of my family and friends, thank you for your love, friendship, and encouragement during the writing of this book. Your prayers and support mean everything to me. You have no idea how important these were and continue to be today.

Wendy Bender, Inspire Ministry Team. Thank you for your friendship, inspiring words, and encouragement during the writing of this book. Your prayers and friendship means everything to me.

Matt Hall, PA, Onsted Family Care and his wonderful team. Thank you for your dedication and reliable care year after year. My family and I always know that when unexpected health issues strike, we can rely on you to receive the best care possible. You are appreciated, and we are so grateful to you.

Dr. Lawrence J. Desjarlais, MD and your team – You all went above and beyond in offering your special services. We would not be where we are today without your loving support. Thank you, too, for your enthusiasm for this book. It could not have happened without you.

Thanks to James A. Auberle MD, Dr. Michael A. Nagel, MD, Rachel Van Viel, CNP, Dr. William Bingaman, and all of their incredible staffs. This whole process was rife with a variety of health ailments along the way. Your support of my writing during this time means the world to me. You went far above and beyond to make me and my family as comfortable as possible. Your kindness is priceless.

A Special Thank You

I count it an honor and a blessing to work with my brother and sister in Christ, Tony and Lynn Marino and their staff at the Alive in Christ Radio Network (AliveinChristRadio.com). They have a passion to reach each hurting soul for Jesus Christ and to see this world changed by becoming ALIVE in His Name. This book simply would not have been possible without their prayers, love, talents, and support. Thank you Tony for your creative direction on the book cover as well as your expertise in marketing and promotion. I also love your crazy sense of humor; you made me laugh when I wanted to cry.

Lynn, I can't thank you enough for your help in the writing of this book. When we wrote it was like our souls were connected as one. You wrote what my soul wanted to say. You are truly a "holy" ghost writer. I also want to thank you for the amazing kitchen tea-towels you gave me. What an amazing testimony of how our Lord works. Before your grandmother passed away in 2001, she embroidered this set of towels with bluebirds and pink flowers on them. Though given as a gift to you, you found it in your heart to give them to me as a reminder of my precious Jaelynn. I believe that this is a true testament of how our glorious Lord works in our lives. He knew we were destined to meet and as you said, your grandmother made these towels for me. Thank you my dear sister in Christ, they will serve as a reminder of our special bond. I will cherish them; forever.

Introduction

You can write a book. This is a statement that many people would find unbelievable. After all, don't you have to be famous or have an extraordinary story? Well yes, but you already do. Everyone's life is unique, but can be an inspiration to others as I hope mine is for you. I may not be famous and I never thought I had the gift of writing, but I do have a story. My life experiences have taught me how to fully lean on Christ. God has shown me over the last twenty-three years, through my sometimes unexplainable, graceful-led journey; that out of ashes He can create beauty and bring honor and glory where it is due; to Jesus Christ, and He can do the same for you.

I was first called to write this book back in March of 2016 when I woke in the middle of the night hearing the words "Glorified Un-Expectations." I kept a notebook on my night stand to jot down thoughts as I was inspired. So, I wrote these two words down and left it at that. A couple of days later, my husband Rick explained that he had a dream the night before in which God had taken him back to one of the hospital incidents with our son Elijah. He said that God had revealed to him that I needed to write a book. That evening, as Rick and I were sitting at the table, a feeling of uncertainty flooded my thoughts; I was still not convinced that writing a book was part of Jesus's plan for my life. As if sensing my reluctance, Rick reminded me that we did not go through all we had for nothing. Suddenly, out of nowhere, I immediately recalled those two words that I had written in the notebook two days earlier; Glorified Un-Expectations. I then heard the Lord speak to me; "Write the words Glorified Un-Expectations and study it." So that's what I did.

In obedience to God, I set out to discover the meaning behind these Words "Glorified Un-Expectations." The Word "glorify" means to honor with praise, admiration, or worship. The "ied" suffix is past tense defining the word glorified as honoring, praising, and worshiping Jesus in the past. UN means "not." Expectation is defined as something that is planned or will happen or be the case in the future. Adding an "s" makes it plural, meaning, many. Therefore, Glorified Un-Expectations is defined as events happening that are not expected which deserve honor, praise, admiration, and worship. Many of those unexpected moments, through joy or sorrow, the glory, honor, and praise of Jesus, is being revealed as He provides His strength to help overcome and rise above the unexpected. No matter what, everything is going to be okay because Jesus is involved. Excitement filled the room. I had just received the meaning behind those two words written in my notebook on my night stand. This was to be the title of the book.

For some strange reason, I kept staring at the Word Un-Expectations. It didn't look right to me, so I looked up the meaning. To my surprise, it's not a word. As I slowly raised my head from embarrassment, I was caught off guard by the words I heard spoken by Rick, "You can't change the title. Jesus gave you the title. It doesn't matter if it's not in the dictionary. The world may say it's an error, but Jesus reminds us we are not to be of this world." That was not only a true statement, but biblical as well, as Romans 12:2 proclaims, *"Do not conform to the pattern of this world, but be transformed by the renewing of your mind. Then you will be able to test and approve what God's will is—His pleasing and perfect will"* (NIV). I believed it was His will that I write this book, but how was I going to do it? With faith!

A few days later, I remember looking out my living room window, and suddenly to my surprise, I find myself talking to Jesus when He reminded me that without faith, one can't climb a mountain. I now understood what my mountain was. My mountain was writing Glorified Un-Expectations. God didn't just call me, He is calling everyone; yes, even you. Jesus has allowed circumstances to happen in your life, both good and bad and He wants you to use what He has allowed for His glory.

My story and His message for you, through me, is one of faith, hope, and love. He has taught me these most amazing attributes through my three beloved children, Jacob, Elijah, and Jaelynn. As you read my story, I pray that you will find faith in Christ as I have. Without Him, I would not be the person I am today. It is faith that has allowed me to not only climb mountains but to move them. When I saw something, including writing this book as impossible, He made it happen. But having and practicing faith can be challenging.

Matthew 17:20 explains how we can move mountains by faith; it reads, *"Because you have so little faith. Truly I tell you, if you have faith as small as a mustard seed, you can say to this mountain, 'Move from here to there,' and it will move. Nothing will be impossible for you"* (NIV). What we must understand is that God is going to give us the desires of our heart as long as they are in accordance with His good and perfect will. Often, we pray to our Heavenly Father asking for what we want whether it is healing, a better job, an improved relationship, or a number of other possibilities only to find that we don't get the answer that we want.

God opens doors and He closes them. We may hear words we do not anticipate or do not want to hear leaving us wondering, but God is still in control. He does not always give us the answer we expect, but we must still praise His glorious grace. God's words will give you what you need, though your faith is weak and small, His strength is all you need; for when we are weak, He is strong. Isaiah 49:29 states, *"He gives strength to the weary and increases the power of the weak"* (NIV). The thought of moving mountains is unimaginable; you can't even see the top from the bottom. Climbing it is a feat, much less moving it. But we must remember what Jesus says in His Word in Psalm 121:1-2, *"I lift up my eyes to the mountains; where does my help come from? My help comes from the Lord, the Maker of heaven and earth"* (NIV). All things are possible in Christ who strengthens us. Through my faith, I have learned to climb and move mountains and you can too.

I was now convinced that writing this book was, in fact, part of God's plan. However, in my humanness I still wondered how it was going to be accomplished, but because of what was being poured out of

God's goodness and my brokenness, I believe God was saying to me to be still and listen to Him. I remember hearing so loudly; "Trust me, it's already written." Jesus needed me with His strength to go back to the place where I thought He had left me, and listen to what my ears could NOW hear. The place where it felt like my world; my life; was falling apart. Even though Jesus was always present and filling me with what was needed to get through each day; He was asking me to walk that same path where unexpectedly, healing had already begun.

During the writing process and moments of uncertainty, He brought to light unexpected and uncomfortable reactions; not to harm me, but to prepare me for this next step. There were days when my thoughts would get the best of me and with many tears not just occasionally but every day, I would ask myself, "Why me?" What's so different about my story than any other story? Everyone has a story to tell about how Jesus has brought them through something. Through His glorious grace He has given me the strength and the ability to stand strong sharing my story and not allowing me to hide from the pain. He knew that I would need to cling to Him with every part of my soul because it was going to be written, published, and exposed.

God told me that I was to write a book for His glory alone. Did I believe it at the time of the revelation? No. I even said no. But no matter what I say, His plan oversees all, and He has shown me daily what exactly He wants my readers to hear. It's a FAITH calling. He is revealing to me that His ways are higher than my ways. Isaiah 55:8-9 reads, *"For my thoughts are not your thoughts, neither are your ways my ways, declares the LORD. For as the heavens are higher than the earth, so are my ways higher than your ways and my thoughts than your thoughts"* (ESV). He is unexpectedly, guiding my hand, and is bringing to life His Words that He alone wants me to include in His book, "Glorified Un-Expectations."

I stand amazed. It's what He is doing through the unexpected, and His glory is written all over the unknown because He is the One to be known. If I had known what His plan was, I would have prepared, right? I would have been ready to fight this raging "back and forth" mentality of inadequacy, and this negative force that tried to take me away from what God has called and equipped me to do. I would have been ready for the battle that God allowed for such a time to help me realize and "live out" God's Word as we read in Isaiah 41:10, "*So do not fear, for I am with you; do not be dismayed, for I am your God. I will strengthen you and help you; I will uphold you with my righteous right hand*"(NIV). He didn't just choose me. He chose you. You are created with a passion and a story. Take that passionate story that Jesus is writing in your life, and let it change you.

Life begins with a story. Your story is His story. Glorified Un-Expectations is written to share with others that when unexpected moments occur, whether through joy or sorrow, Jesus is doing something far greater than we can comprehend that will, in His timing, reveal His Glory. We may not understand right now, but He does, and all He wants me to do is trust Him by putting my faith in Him as He shows me step by step how to write the story He has known from the very beginning; a story that was written unexpectedly; Glorified Un-Expectations.

Trusting Christ

I know I have stated over and over, God has not only called me, but He is calling you too. He has allowed events in your life, both good and bad to happen so that He may be glorified, but only if you let Him. He wants to use these events in your life to encourage and uplift others so that HE may be glorified. It is easy to praise God when our lives are going smoothly, but what about when the road gets rough. Do you blame Him for the bad things that are happening or do you still praise His glorious grace? After all, nowhere in the bible does it say that once we accept Christ and become born again will we live the rest of our lives in a fairy tale existence. What He truly wants is a relationship with us. He wants us to rely upon Him and trust Him in all aspects of our lives.

Prayer is a communication with God, and when we pray we must trust His answer. But what about the times where you prayed with faith, believing that He would provide the answer and everything would be fine and you get nothing. You know God is in control, but nothing. Do you give up on God? No, you must realize that He has heard your prayer, but His answer may be "no," or "not yet." We must remember that God's timing is not our timing. He knows what's best for us. Often times we pray when life is hardest. Loss is very hard, I know. I've been there. You may say words like, "I want my answer now; God I trusted You; I asked for more faith. Isn't that what You want us to have? Give me more faith so my worry will turn to joy. God I've read Your Word and how having faith as small as a mustard seed can move mountains. That's very tiny. God, you want me to have little faith? Say to this mountain, move, and it will move with little faith? Move a mountain? No way, that's huge. But though we may have little faith; we have a bigger God. God's Word tells us in 2 Corinthians 12:9 *"My grace is sufficient for you, for my power is made perfect in weakness"* (NIV). He will give you what you need, though your faith is weak and small, His strength is all you need; for when I am weak, You God, are strong. You can't have faith without God, and having faith is trusting in Him. Without Jesus, I am nothing. Every day, I must continually learn and choose to trust in Jesus and His Word that He proclaims in 1 Corinthians 13:13, *"And now these three remain: faith, hope, and love. But the greatest of these is love"* (NIV).

Faith, Hope, and Love – Once you experience their power, they can change your life forever. This is my story, all for His glory, Amen.

FAITH

Jacob's Story

Motherhood is one of the most joyful occasions in a woman's life; and one of the most natural. It is our task as we are told in Genesis 9:7 to, *"Be fruitful and multiply"* (NIV). It is also our responsibility to *"Start a child in the way he should go"* as we read in Proverbs, 22:6 (NIV). In fact, the bible is the perfect parenting guide telling us precisely how our children should be raised. What is more interesting however is what I have learned from my children about the kingdom of God. The Lord has blessed me with three beautiful children yet each has proven to be an exercise in practicing my own Christianity.

I call Jacob my faith child because of what I have learned about my faith through him. Few little girls grow up professing that they want to grow up to be a teen mom. However, this very experience started me on a journey that would lead to many truths about faith.

For example, once Jacob was born, I prayed that the Lord would bring Jacob and I a man who could be the spiritual leader of our home; a man who loved his wife as the church (Ephesians 5:25) and would be a Godly example for my son. I often questioned who would want a young woman who already had a child. But believing in prayer, God did indeed bring the right man into our lives. Rick and I went on to have two more children, but this is Jacobs's story and how my faith has grown because of what God has done through him. I hope that it inspires you to look at your own children and listen to what the Lord may be teaching you as you teach your child to love Jesus.

Graduating Pregnant

It was the first day of August, 1990 and the day had been sunny and beautiful. Having just graduated from high school, I was ready to take on the world, ready to take on anything; anything, including raising a baby boy as a single teenage parent. The night Jacob was born, I remember my parents driving me to the hospital. I had a myriad of emotions floating through my mind, body and even my very soul. What would the future hold? How was I going to parent this child when I was still a child myself? Who was going to take care of us and most importantly, what did the future hold for my dear sweet child who was soon to be born? As I contemplated these questions, I gazed out of the car window and looked up into the night sky. Looking at the brightly lit stars a wave of peace soothed my soul. The stars that illuminated the sky represented a sense of hope reminding me that no matter what I may face in life, there will always be something, or someone, to help guide the way. In this case, the stars in the heavens gave me that hope.

Jacob is Born

After many hours of intense labor, a beautiful little boy came into this world weighing 7 pounds and 6 ounces, with a full head of brown hair. When his big brown eyes met mine, I knew that very moment no matter how difficult raising my baby would be, he would know that he had a mommy who would nurture and care for him forever.

Once baby Jacob arrived, it was time to introduce him to his new grandparents, family, and friends. I so wanted my parents to be ecstatic - as Jacob was their first grandson. He was the only boy in the family that would grow up to carry on the "Eaton" name. I wanted my parents to be proud of my precious new child and proud of their nineteen-year-old who would be saying goodbye to her youth and hello to a lifetime commitment as a new mother. However, they were nervous as well, unsure about what the future held for their little girl and her newborn. They knew this was certainly going to change my life, but theirs as well. Parents naturally want to protect their children from making negative choices in life. In this case, they were not only protecting me, they were also protecting their grandson. They did what parents do best. They loved me unconditionally, and I was determined to do the same for my son.

Teenage Single Parent

Being a single parent can affect you spiritually and emotionally. There were many days of rain. Not rain from heaven but tears that streamed down the face of a young mother who was unaware of where her life was going. I can't say that I was all alone. Thankfully, I had very supportive parents.

Searching and Seeking

Jacob and I learned together. I was his mommy, and he was my son. Here I was, a young mother just out of high school and raising a child. My role was to teach him and provide for him so that he would survive in this big world that he was coming to know. Anyone who has had the honor of raising a child knows it is not an easy task. I was learning quickly just how true that is – it is NOT easy! As I held Jacob in my arms it brought clarity to my mind. Not only was I responsible for my own life, I had the responsibility of taking care of another person. This left me searching for more. I recall a time when I was in my room crying and feeling so alone. Fear of the unknown started to surface. What have I done? Will my little boy ever have a daddy to love him? Who would want to date a young woman who already had a child? I wanted my little boy to experience the best that this world had to offer. I didn't want him to go through life without a daddy. Though I had made misguided choices which brought this child into the world, I did not want him to suffer for it. I needed a godly man in my life to lead this family. I felt empty, but knew that there was something more.

Wanting to raise my child in the best way possible, I turned to Jesus. Up until this time, I knew about Him, but I did not know Him.

Faithful Praying

I can recall a time when I would often think and say to myself that there has got to be something more to this life; this is when I read Romans 8:1 which says, "*Therefore, there is now no condemnation for those who are in Christ Jesus*" (NIV). A moment later, I heard little footsteps coming towards my room. It was Jacob. He came over to me, and placed his little hands on my back and said with a smile, "Mommy, don't cry. God will give us a daddy to love us. It's going to be okay." Three years old, and Jacob was comforting me, when I was supposed to be comforting him. He brings so much joy into my life. He showed me an example of "childlike faith" and what it's all about. Through this and many other experiences together, we came to know the truth, and found a daddy to take care of us. A daddy we call our Heavenly Father, Jesus Christ. Titus 3:5 says, "*He saved us, not because of righteous things we had done, but because of his mercy. He saved us through the washing of rebirth and renewal by the Holy Spirit*" (NIV). In Galatians 2:20 we read, "*I have been crucified with Christ and I no longer live, but Christ lives in me. The life I now live in the body, I live by faith in the Son of God, who loved me and gave Himself for me*" (NIV).

Not only did I come to know parenthood, I came to know so much more. I was learning to live by faith. John 6:45 tells us, "*As it is written in Scripture, 'they will all be taught by God. Everyone who listens to the Father and learns from Him comes to me'*" (NLT).

Children's Bible Reading

As Jacob and I clung to Jesus, I found myself asking questions like, "How do I know I am a child of God?" There was a hunger to just sit and read His Word, not with the knowledge of the world but using the gift I received when I gave my life to Christ; the Holy Spirit. I had heard only a little bit about the Bible, and I remember just wanting to know everything I could about this inspiring book, but when I picked it up, I really didn't understand it; all the numbers, different chapters, red letters, etc. In an attempt to gain understanding I went to my local Christian book store and moseyed my way to the children's book aisle and looked for a picture bible that I could start out with. This was perfect. It was colorful, exciting, and I could see what was happening. This is where I began studying the Bible and learning about how to live a life for Christ.

As I was learning about the Bible, I wanted Jacob to learn too so I involved him in the AWANA program at a local church. AWANA is a program that stands for 'Approved Workmen Are Not Ashamed.' This program provides spiritual principals for preschoolers, ages 3 – 5, by helping them develop respect for God, His Son, and His Word. He would come home from the meetings and be so excited about reciting new verses. Each week they would have to learn verses for the following meeting. If they were able to recite the verse, they would receive a gem to add to their crown which was worn on their cubbies vest. I still have his vest safely packed away along with other precious memories.

Now Do You Believe?

That evening, the unexpected occurred. I remember hearing four Words, "Now, do you believe?" and then waking up from a dream in the early morning hours. These words were so powerful to me that they awakened my heart to know Jesus does answer prayer. He also answers in His timing and His way. He knew my deepest desire was to know all I could about who this God was and how life has meaning when you accept Him as your personal Savior. As I fell back to sleep, a vision came into view. It was as if I were looking down from the sky, into an open church sanctuary filled with pews where parishioners worship their God. I was sitting in one of the pews crying and I had my hands cradled in my lap, afraid to look up. I knew it was me, and I knew that there was evil surrounding me.

My thoughts could not recollect how and why this was happening. As I looked up to the front, the voice behind the pew was cursing God and ranting all sorts of vulgarity. "No! This can't be! Why am I here? Where are you God?" Suddenly, as my face was still cradled in my lap, tears falling to the floor, I glance down to my left and notice feet with sandals and a white robe walking down the aisle. Not even looking up, my spirit sensed peace. I did not see a face. All I could see was a hand that was reaching for mine, and hearing a voice saying, "Come with Me."

As I stood up, I felt a hand reach for my hand and gently led me peacefully to the front of the podium where evil was present. He gently raised my hand towards this figure and speaks "Satan, be gone," and with a voice so confident and reassuring said, "Now, do you believe?" Immediately, I sat up in bed not knowing what just took place. Did this really happen? God just dismissed the devil with the wave of a hand. We can do the same as we learn in James 4:7, "*Submit yourselves, then, to God. Resist the devil and he will flee from you*" (NIV). I continued to ask God, "Was this Your way of answering my prayer that I am a child of God?" I didn't know what to take from this. I was just learning all about Jesus and thought to myself, how nice that when I ask Jesus something, He answers. Jacob and I began to learn how we could go to our Heavenly Father and pray for anything we asked for in His Name, for John 14:14 tells us, "*You can ask for anything in my name, and I will do it, so that the Son can bring glory to the Father*"(NLT).

Learning to Live by Faith

To live by faith was not an overnight process. It took time for me to really believe that life was going to be okay for my son and me. Did I doubt? Yes. Did I have fear? Yes. These feelings did not go away, and it scared me. Now that I had accepted Jesus, what's next? Does my life automatically change instantly? I found out my answer shortly thereafter because those feelings of the unknown resurfaced. What I had come to know from accepting Jesus was that my past, present, and future sins are forgiven. I am a new person. My old ways are gone and now I am a new person. Romans 6:6, "*For we know that our old self was crucified with Him so that the body ruled by sin might be done away with, that we should no longer be slaves to sin*"(NIV).

I have the power in my Spirit to overcome those negative feelings that try to destroy what Jesus has freed me from. He gave me the gift of the Holy Spirit. I can now live with security. Before accepting Jesus, I was not capable of even understanding the peace that comes with knowing Him because I didn't know Him as I do today. When I accepted Jesus Christ as my personal Savior I thought that seriously my life would be smooth sailing. Now that I had said "yes" I thought that I was in the "safe and shallow zone." What I did not realize is that He was teaching me how to depend and rely on Him through faith, for there were many trials that lay ahead that only faith would get me through.

Second Date

Jacob and I prayed every day asking Jesus for a daddy and a man to come into our lives and love us. After faithfully praying for four years, our prayer was finally answered. God brought into our life a man that would love me for who I was, and Jacob as his own son. God brought to us Rick Daniels. From the very beginning, Rick accepted Jacob as his own son. On our second date, he asked if Jacob could come along. Now that is a special man! As I fell in love with him it was like I was looking directly into the eyes of Jesus. Rick was most definitely a gift from God.

As the months passed by, Rick, Jacob and I would spend as much time together as possible. One of my fondest memories are the days we spent at Devil's Lake where there was an outdoor Christian theater. We would go, spread a blanket on the grass and enjoy the evenings. It would be many years later that Jacob would have his senior pictures taken at this very park. Just nine short months later, Rick would ask me to marry him.

The Ring

We became a family on September 19th, 1998. In planning our wedding, we wanted to do something special for Jacob to let him know that we were becoming a family. At the reception, we gave him a ring that represented one unit, one family. I gained a wonderful husband and Jacob gained a loveable daddy. It was the four of us; Jesus, Daddy, Mommy, and Jacob.

Honeymoon Chaos

The smooth sailing waters soon ended and we were in over our heads because when we arrived back from our honeymoon, I ended up getting very sick. The plane ride caused my sinuses to block resulting in a severe sinus infection. After x-rays, the doctor's confirmed that sometime in my past I had broken my nose and it caused a deviated septum. This would involve surgery to remove cartilage and fix the problem. I felt so bad for my husband; all I could think about was how draining this would be for Rick. When the pastor said in sickness and health, I guess we would find out much sooner than expected just how dedicated he would be. However, being the man of integrity that he is, he was so good to me. He took care of me and I felt safe. When we were dating, we would have long talks about some very emotional times in my life, and the things I had experienced, which left me scared and unsure. He would always remind me and tell me I never had to be afraid again, because he would be my guardian angel, and he would take care of me; and that he did. I thank Jesus every day for bringing Rick into my life. I am so grateful for Rick's love and dedication to me and Jacob.

The Tiny Bedroom

Having a blended family has its challenges with so many changes. Before we married, Jacob and I lived with my parents. My mom and dad were like a second parent to Jacob. Their home was his home. Jacob's nursery was my bedroom in my parents' house. We had a little corner for his beautiful bassinet with a baby-blue sailboat comforter, perfect for a baby boy with a little pillow to lay his head. We made it our own and I was so grateful to have such supportive parents. During our wedding planning days, we knew we had to have a place to live so Rick and I planned to buy a modular home and place it on some of the farm land that his parents gave to us as a gift for our wedding.

Here's a tip for newlyweds, do not plan a wedding and build a house during the same time. We had the opportunity to design our home so we could choose where we wanted the nursery. This nursery served as Jacob's bedroom because the upstairs was not completed upon moving in after the honeymoon. I am so thankful that Jacob could use this bedroom. I remember thinking when it was just him and I, will I ever be able to provide for him and give him everything a child deserves; a place to protect him, a place he can call his own. It felt right because I wanted to be close to Jacob. To me, this was his nursery that I was not able to give him at the time, and as I think back at this memory, his bed was in the corner of our new home because that was all the room we had. This room was tiny. We have had many laughs over this. Jacob had so many things he had to get used to; a new home, a new school, new friends. Jacob adjusted as best as he could.

Step-Father and Son Bonding

The first year we learned to bond together as a family. It was difficult for Jacob to adjust to his new home and the open space that the good ol' country provides. One exciting memory that Jacob has always remembered is being able to go to a full week camp, away from mom and dad. Back in Rick's college day's he was a camp counselor at Spring Hill in Evart Michigan, a well-known Evangelical Christian camp for kids of all ages with a strong message of salvation. Jacob would attend not just one summer but several, and he really looked forward to these times. He was able to share his experience with those of Ricks thus their bond strengthened.

In later years as Jacob was entering high school he began to show great interest in sports, especially track. Rick had also participated in track and in fact, held the record for the fastest runner at Sand Creek High School. Ironically, Jacob attended the very same school and was able to participate on the very team Rick had; it was as if he was following in Rick's footsteps. Jacob had even been featured on the front of our daily telegram which brought back memories for Rick.

As we all adjusted to our new family Jacob was turning nine. Rick and I decided that we wanted to have a baby together and share the joy of having a brother or sister for Jacob. In the fall of 1999, we became pregnant. The news brought a lot of joy to our family and we were so excited.

A Birthday Celebration

We were still in the hospital with new baby Elijah on Jacob's birthday, August 1st, so we decided to have a little party in the lobby for him to celebrate his day. Despite the chaos and difficulties going on around him, Jacob showed so much strength and he accepted every obstacle with a smile on his face. I was so proud of him for showing us his love for his new baby brother Elijah. We even had the spray streamers to surprise him. I doubt any nine-year-old would want to have their birthday in the hospital, but under the circumstances, Jacob made the best of it and was a real trooper. It was such a great time, even in a hospital setting.

By definition, faith is believing in what you cannot see. In the Bible, Jesus speaks of faith in Hebrews 11:1, *"Faith is the confidence that what we hope for will actually happen; it gives us assurance about things we cannot see"* (NLT). This is not an easy concept. As humans we constantly want proof that something is real or has merit. It is natural to doubt and for many of us it creeps into our mind when it is least wanted or needed. To remain faithful, we must keep our eyes focused on Jesus and what his Word says in 1 Peter 5:8, *"Stay alert! Watch out for your great enemy, the devil. He prowls around like a roaring lion, looking for someone to devour"* (NLT). This same enemy will continually torment us with thoughts of inadequacy and incompetence, leading us to believe that we are insignificant in this world. But in God's world we have great worth and value and can accomplish much. I found this to be true in raising Jacob. Anyone who is a parent knows what a challenge it can be. However, for a young and scared mother, without faith it would have proven to be insurmountable. As my knowledge in our loving Father grew, so did my faith. I believed that the Lord would provide the perfect man and father for me and Jacob. I believed that, *"Jesus had a perfect plan for me, a plan to not hurt me; a plan to prosper me and not to harm me, a plan to give me a hope and a future,"* as I learned in Jerimiah 29:11 (NIV). I continue to cling to His many promises through His Word. As I do, my faith continues to grow.

Praying for our children is a regular practice for the Christian parent. As you watch your children grow, allow your faith in God to grow as well. God says that if we ask in His name, it will be given to us; *"Ask and it will be given to you; seek and you will find; knock and the door will be opened to you"* (Matthew 7:7, NIV). Therefore, we should continue to pray for our children expecting that our loving Lord will in fact bring good gifts. And finally, we can hope. When we hope we have an expectation and a desire for something unexpected yet wonderful to happen. At this point in our lives, Rick, Jacob and I hoped to expand our family and God blessed us with yet another member to our family. With Elijah, I learned about hope.

HOPE

Elijah's Story

I have read numerous definitions for hope. In fact, if you Google the word, "hope" you will come up with over 131 million hits. But the simplest way I have found to describe the word is, "an expectation of positive outcomes in regard to life events and circumstances." We all want to live fairytale lives where nothing bad ever happens. We dream of days filled with perfect health, full bank accounts, and loving family and friends where conflict does not exist. In reality our days are filled with stress and worry as our health deteriorates, the economy crashes and conflict between humans is more common than a cat's meow. For those without Christ, it can become so overwhelming that even the thought of living another day can become surmountable.

Everyone suffers, even Christians. Often, we believe that once we accept Christ the fairytale life will become a reality where every day is filled with perfect houses, perfect children, and perfect marriages which is far from the truth. Everyone still struggles with everyday maladies and must learn to handle situations. Our Lord never promised that life would be easy even with Him. *"Peace I leave with you; my peace I give you. I do not give to you as the world gives. Do not let your hearts be troubled and do not be afraid"* (John 14:27, NIV). But as Christians what we now have that was illusive before knowing Him is hope. Without Christ, life can be too much to bear. Hopelessness sets in and we find ourselves weak, depressed, and even in extreme cases suicidal. But Christ tells us in Mark 9:23, *"Everything is possible for one who believes"* (NLT). Therefore, we have hope despite the trials and tribulations we may experience. In fact, many of the most difficult times of our lives become the best life lessons.

Many people believe that as a parent if they share their mistakes with their children that the kids will believe that if mom (or dad) did it, it must be ok. You often see this in behaviors. A parent who smokes will have a difficult time teaching their own children not to do the same. Modeling is very important and another reason we should learn to live like Christ; so that we can model Christ for our own children. That stated some mistakes can be learning lessons not only for us, but for others as well. For example, I made choices which resulted in becoming a teen parent. At this point I had to face how to deal with the situation and chose to have my baby despite the difficulties I would experience as an unmarried, teen mom. I can't imagine any parent would be proud of their child for making choices which lead to teen pregnancy, yet unless we are engaged with our children, they are likely to repeat our mistakes, thinking it must be acceptable behavior.

As humans we will continually make mistakes. However, how we handle them is what makes the biggest difference not only in our lives, but in those surrounding us. When I became pregnant with Jacob, I felt hopelessness. I thought my life was over before it even had a chance to begin. Thankfully, this situation helped me turn to Christ. Through faith I accepted Christ and He took a situation that could have destroyed me and turned it into good. In fact, Romans 8:28 tells us, *"And we know that God works all things together for the good of those who love Him, who are called according to His purpose"* (NIV). Accepting Christ gave me a new purpose and I wanted to become more like Him. Through faith, I found hope.

Hope is a beautiful thing. Without it we find despair. One of the greatest symbols of hope is the birth of a new child. We are so excited about the prospect of bringing another life into the world and we are not only willing but excited to give up ourselves for that new, tiny, bundle of joy. In fact, becoming a parent is an excellent lesson in unconditional love. We now sacrifice our own comforts for those of our child. How many of you have had sleepless nights, cold meals, and spit-up stained clothes all in the name of tending to the needs of a precious new child. Having a newborn is hard work even for an easy baby. But what if the new child is born with complications, or is destined to live a life of difficulty due to health issues?

Stress and worry are normal for any parent but compounded when there are complications. Every parent professes that they only want their child to be healthy, born with 10 fingers and 10 toes. But what if they are born without a hand, or have a cleft pallet? Do we love them less? No; of course not. But without Christ, these problems are compounded. Without hope, we have nothing but despair. Elijah is my hope baby. Through him I have learned to lean on Christ even during the worst of times. Bringing Elijah into this world was troublesome as I had a difficult pregnancy. After his birth the challenges continued to the point Rick and I dropped to our knees and released him to Jesus. Making it through some very troubling times, we have found so much joy in this child. Elijah is my hope baby; this is his story.

Expecting

In October of 1999, we received the wonderful news that we were expecting. This was a very exciting time for me because I not only was expecting a child; my prayer of giving Jacob a sibling was coming true, and I was going to be able to experience this joyous moment with a husband. It was so exciting to see my belly grow each day and I remember just being so thankful for every moment.

Bed Rest

During one of our regular doctor visits, the nurse took my blood pressure and noticed that upon standing it would rise and become dangerously high. So, at five months, the doctor ordered me to bed rest until the time of delivery, allowing better blood flow for Elijah. Lying in bed, day in and day out, only being able to get up to go to the bathroom proved to be very difficult. I felt fine physically, but felt guilty knowing there was much work to be done that fell on the shoulders of Rick and Jacob and other family members. But it had to be done so I could deliver a healthy baby.

During another appointment, I was quietly and peacefully listening to my baby's heartbeat. Suddenly, a nurse came running in and told Rick that my blood pressure was extremely high and rising and the baby was in distress. Again, the fear of the unknown crept in, but this time, I wasn't alone. I had God and a loving, supportive husband by my side. An ambulance was called to transport me to a special hospital that was equipped with the necessary equipment that may be needed in case of a premature delivery.

A Delivery of Hope, Elijah is Born

With faith and hope holding us together, we gave birth to a beautiful baby boy. On April 13, 2000, Elijah Richard Daniels was born weighing in at 2 pounds 10 ounces and was 15 inches long. He was so tiny, his skin translucent, not yet ready to come into this world. Though I so badly wanted to hold him, I was not able to. He had to be put in an incubator immediately after deliver which was protocol for a child born prematurely. All I cared about was that he was breathing and alive. The doctors gave us the news that we were not out of danger, and at this stage, anything could happen. Baby Elijah needed to buy time and grow.

Stay in the NICU

Elijah was immediately admitted to the NICU (Neonatal Intensive Care Unit) where doctors and nurses could care for him constantly. How can this be? I have a child at home who needs me! How am I going to take care of Jacob and Elijah at the same time? At that moment, I can remember how unsure I felt. My emotions were everywhere. I didn't know what to feel. I was happy because I had just delivered a baby boy, and sad because this meant that the next few months I would be away from my other child, Jacob. I was so confused.

Many adjustments would have to take place in the next few months. Rick's parents as well as mine offered to take care of Jacob while we were in the hospital. As I gained my strength after a successful delivery, I remember being wheeled down a long hallway. I didn't even know what to expect. The nurse took us into this little room with a gigantic stainless-steel sink with yellow gowns hanging up beside it. Not very stylish I would say to myself but they did serve their purpose. Every visitor that came to visit would have to wear one of these gowns to prevent the spread of germs.

The moment I have been waiting for, that normal nine months had finally arrived. I was going to meet my baby for the first time. I walked into a very spacious room. I could see parents clinging close to what looked like large plastic tubs with two small holes in the side. Some people were crying. Some were smiling. Some were just there. No expression. As I came closer to my own plastic tub, reality hit me and tears swelled up in my eyes. This was more than just a plastic tub. This was where my baby's life began. Beside his incubator was a rocking chair.

Oh, how I wanted to take Elijah in my arms and hold him and keep him safe and secure in his mommy's arms. But I could not hold him yet. The safest place for Elijah to be right now was inside the incubator. Hearing this news was very difficult to accept but I had no choice but to agree. I found myself getting as close to the tub as I possibly could. There were two small holes on the side of the incubator which served a great purpose. I could place my hands inside and touch my baby's tiny arm, letting him know that his mommy was there and that it wouldn't be long before he would be safely at home where his big brother and the rest of his loving family were waiting.

Ronald McDonald Hospitality

For Rick and me, our home away from home became the Ronald McDonald House. This charitable organization provides families who are dealing with sick children a place to stay so they can be close to their children. Not only did we receive support from the staff, we also were in close contact with other families who were going through trying times as well. I will never forget the hospitality that the Ronald McDonald House offered to our family. Whenever we treat ourselves to McDonalds, those change holders that are located below the cashier window serve as a reminder of how thankful we are to have had a place like the Ronald McDonald House.

Home Sweet Home

It was now July and after 3 ½ months in the NICU we were ready to take our precious bundle of joy home. When we arrived home from the hospital we couldn't have been happier. I remember coming home in the evening, pulling into the driveway and seeing a "welcome home" sign hanging on the door. As Rick opened the car door, I looked down and grabbed the preemie car seat that the hospital provided us. This car seat was special as it allowed Elijah at just 4.8 pounds to lie down while connected to the tangle of cords attached to the monitor. The doctor shared with us that babies this small tend to stop breathing, so the alarm from the device would alert us if that were to happen with Elijah. The cords would remain on Elijah until he could live without any episodes of any frightening health risks.

With the car seat and monitor in my hands, we walked into our home with our little bundle of joy for the first time. It was wonderful. Big brother Jacob was the first to see Elijah. Our mothers and fathers as well as great grandpa Ezra came over to hold their newest grandson. As I watched them hold him, a smile came to my face, and I couldn't help but again, thank Jesus because He gave us this moment, this evening, with no alarms, no beeps, no doctors, just family, the way it was meant to be.

Head Growing Faster Than Body

Elijah was very fragile so we stayed home the first couple of weeks. It was difficult taking him places and home was the best place for him.

Our excitement of being home gradually diminished as Elijah began showing signs of stress. Weeks went by and we noticed he would cry every time we placed him on his back. This was not a cry because of a wet diaper or feeling hungry. This was different. My motherly instinct was kicking in and all I wanted to do was have him with me. He seemed to be content when sleeping on my chest, so we did this for about a week. One day as I was lying in bed with Elijah on my chest, I heard a silent voice say, "You need to call your pediatrician." Without hesitation, I picked up the phone and called the pediatrician; he agreed to see him that day.

I remember it was almost closing time and as I was in the doctor's office, I watched as he took out a measuring device and measured Elijah's head. The doctor looked at me with eyes telling me this was not good. I suddenly heard the doctor say, "You need to get Elijah to the hospital. His head is growing faster than his body." I was alone at the time and I didn't even remember calling Rick, because all I kept hearing was the word hospital. Time just stopped and the next thing I knew Rick was beside me and we were driving to the hospital that was not just a few minutes away. It would take us forty-five minutes to get there.

He's Yours Jesus

When we arrived, we pulled into the emergency department and I ran in with Elijah in my arms. I did not know what to do. The hospital staff had already been informed that we were coming and upon arrival they took him from my arms; I grabbed Rick and just sobbed. The only sounds I could hear was my crying and the doctor telling us that they were going to take a CT scan of Elijah's head.

Minutes turned into hours and finally we saw someone in a white coat come to us with an uncertain look. "Mr. and Mrs. Daniels, we need to take Elijah downstairs to perform an MRI. We see something, but we are not exactly sure what we are dealing with." We got on the elevator and headed down to the MRI scanning room located in the basement of the hospital. After exiting the elevator, we were led down a very dark, long hallway with exposed pipes. We were in the depths of the hospital and no one was there except us and the medical team working with Elijah. As we turned to the left, we could see chairs and a window that looked like a waiting area but with the lights off.

Again, all I remember is grabbing Rick as we slowly lowered ourselves to the ground bowing on bended knee and with hands close to our hearts praying, "Dear Jesus, please help us! Please help us! You see that our son Elijah needs You. We need You. Please heal him Lord." As we were pleading with Jesus to help us, our hearts connected as one; Rick and I looked up into each other's eyes, and before ending our prayer we said, "Father, we give Elijah back to You. He is Your child. You have given him to us and now we give him back to You. Your will be done." We stayed there bowed in silence until we heard the door opening and my heart just froze.

Cancer Scare

The expression on the doctor's face looked more concerned as he came to us requesting that we follow him to where Elijah was lying. As I dried my tears, we bravely walked into the room, taking notice of a monitor screen with an image of three perfectly round cyst-like objects located in his brain. Again, I clutched Rick's arm as my eyes zoomed in on the monitor. The doctor said, "We think there is a possibility that we may be dealing with cancer but we are not certain until we perform emergency brain surgery tomorrow morning. However, something is there and this is our best option." I could not move. I could not even cry. I felt like someone was hitting my heart with a hammer and I could not escape. This would not have been the first time that the word "cancer" had shown its ugly face in our immediate family.

In 1996, before I married Rick, my mother who was only fifty years old was struck with breast cancer. This was a shock to us as cancer does not run in our family. However, we were told by her medical staff to expect the worst; the odds of surviving this ravishing disease were not good. Her treatment began with chemotherapy and radiation which resulted in the dreaded hair loss. Again, our amazing Father turned a bad situation into good as this gave my mom the opportunity to show the love of Jesus to others she encountered in her fight.

During one of her chemo treatments which currently take place every three weeks, I sympathetically asked how she was doing. Her reply, as tears streamed down my face, assured me as well as amused me. She stated, "I'm getting my spa treatment." Anyone who has experienced a "spa treatment" or facial knows how great you feel afterward. There is a radiant glow and it just makes you feel good about yourself. This simple statement proclaimed that no matter what we may face; we can overcome with the strength of Jesus Christ. Miraculously she beat the odds and went into remission. Over the next 21 years, she would go through three more bouts of battling cancer. In 2011 the cancer was back again. This time it spread to her jugular vein and into her lungs. Remarkably, she beat it again.

My mother has become such an inspiration for me as well as anyone she has come into contact with during her "spa treatments." She has used this time and opportunity to encourage others with the love of Christ. Though she is fighting the battle for her life, she never ceases to stop and give thanks and praise to her creator. She remains determined to fight the battle with Jesus as her healer giving Him honor and praise no matter what she may face during this battle. She continues to hold fast to the scripture in Colossians 3:17, *"And whatever you do, whether in word or deed, do it all in the name of the Lord Jesus, giving thanks to God the Father through him"* (NIV).

I always hold on to those beautiful words. She often says, when the valley seems deep, "I may have the big C, but I have a bigger C (Christ) watching over me."

First Brain Surgery

Elijah was scheduled the next morning for brain surgery to remove what the doctors had alarmed us to earlier; the threat of cancer. All I could say was "No, not again. We are not supposed to be here. Why does my baby have to go through more pain? He is only three months old. Why cancer? Jesus, help us!" My mind and soul could not escape the very familiar emotions of doubt and fear. This was not what we were expecting at all. We had just fought for his life in the NICU.

A team of neurologists were called in and we just stared at our little miracle baby in ICU attached to yet another machine; this time a ventilator breathing for him. Water on the brain was causing his head to swell and make his eyes bulge outward. We were then given the devastating news that Elijah was not able to see. Whatever was happening in his brain was causing him to be blind. Did I miss something? Were we not out of danger? All we could do was pray and hope that Jesus had heard our prayer. Morning came as our hearts were crying out to Jesus as He held Elijah. As we watched Elijah's chest rise and fall with every breath, all I wanted to do was hold him and tell him everything was going to be okay.

Pastor Steve Praying

It was early morning and the doctors told us it would be soon that Elijah would be going into surgery. As I stood, I turned around and directly behind me was my pastor, Pastor Steve Van Winkle. I will never forget this moment. Together we prayed right there in the ICU; we lifted Elijah in prayer.

We didn't know how long the surgery would last, but it felt like forever.

Staph Infection

We decided to go to the hospital cafeteria. As we were eating we saw the surgeon come into the cafeteria with great news. He said, "We've got good news, and we have got not so good news. The good news is we are only dealing with abscesses caused by a staph infection. Not cancer. The bad news is that Elijah will have to stay in the hospital another six weeks to be on IV antibiotics." This we can do and once again we found hope. We will spend as much time needed to once again bring him home to where he belonged. Each day Elijah was growing stronger and stronger and we were so thankful for his recovery.

The Vision Test

The doctors found it necessary to test Elijah's eyes. They suspected that the abscesses had caused him to lose his vision, but were not sure of the extent. The last eight weeks in the hospital were exhausting, but we felt all the many prayers offered on Elijah's behalf. In a short time before we left the hospital, we had the best news any parent could receive considering the circumstances. After all the pressure was released, his brain compensated and restored his vision. Our baby would not be blind! However, what was affected was his motor skills and muscle tone. Elijah was very weak.

Special Services

After being released from the hospital Elijah received rehabilitation services from a local clinic that specialized in occupational therapy. They would come to the house every week and work with him. We are very grateful to all the people who helped Elijah get the medical attention he needed during this difficult time. He was doing so well, and we were so proud of him. Again, we found ourselves thanking our faithful Jesus.

Infantile Spasms

One evening when Rick and I were holding Elijah enjoying him coo and smile and looking at him, he suddenly lost control of his head which alarmed us. Once again, we recognized that something was wrong. Elijah would lose control of his head multiple times and his pupils would enlarge. Back to a mother's instinct and this time a father's instinct as well, we called our neurologist and set up an appointment for him to be seen as soon as possible. The doctor was not alarmed in our description of his symptoms telling us that babies do not have control of their heads at this developmental stage. He assured us that we had nothing to worry about. Back at home, we tried our best to focus on just one day at a time. We were so thankful to have our boys safe and healthy at home. After the scare of the abscesses and the assurance of the doctor, we thought for sure we were through the struggles until again; Elijah would lose control of his head. Our instincts told us that this was not normal.

The Video Camera

Rick and I took matters into our own hands and videotaped these episodes. We took the video tape to the neurologist so he could witness firsthand what we were seeing and, yes, he confirmed the unexpected. We were told Elijah was experiencing a rare form of seizure activity called Infantile Spasms. The extent to his treatment would involve a rare drug called ACTH that had to be shipped on ice from California. This drug was a new experimental drug so it was very rare and quite expensive. Without it Elijah may have been wheelchair bound for the rest of his life. However, our faithful Father Jesus made it possible for us to obtain this wonderful gift.

Elijah would need this drug daily so Rick and I were trained on how to administer it. We were to inject the medicine into both of Elijah's tiny little thighs once a day. Rick and I prayed that this new experimental drug would work; without it Elijah's quality of life would suffer. Our lives would be on hold once again, as well as Elijah's developmental state due to the side effects of the medication. His whole body would swell up to the point he was not able to move. He would just lie very still in a vegetative state and we would smile at him with every ounce of strength we had hoping that he would not feel the hopelessness and defeat we were truly feeling. All we wanted was for Elijah to experience somewhat of a normal life considering everything he had gone through up until now.

The next three months were critical. Elijah's immune system was suppressed so we kept him home and out of the public to protect him from contracting any other sickness. This was not easy. It affected all of us, especially Jacob. Jacob would lie on the floor next to his brother and try to make him smile, and when he did Elijah's cheeks would puff up. He was our little pumpkin.

Infantile Treatment Success

Four months later, and with many prayers, we received wonderful news at his neurology appointment. The doctor confirmed that Elijah's treatment was successful and the ACTH had stopped the infantile spasms. We were so thankful. Through many more prayers, and help from our family and friends, we celebrated and overcame the unexpected of this debilitating illness. Once again, we were able to hope for brighter days.

Because you Love Me Gift

My mom and sister wanted to surprise us with a gift as a reminder of how Jesus brought us through another Glorified Un-Expectation with a picture of Elijah when his body was so bloated. Despite the struggle, Elijah had the most joyful smile on his face. The lyrics to a song by Celine Dion, "Because You Loved Me" were written on the front of his picture. Everyone who knows me knows that lyrics speak to me in a powerful way. When I opened the gift, my eyes went directly to Elijah, as tears welled up in my eyes and I began to read...

"You were my strength when I was weak,
You were my voice when I couldn't speak,
You were my eyes when I couldn't see,
You saw the best there was in me,
Lifted me up when I couldn't reach
You gave me faith, because you believed,
I'm everything I am
Because you loved me."

To us, these words represented Jesus pouring His love out to us, bringing us through this pain and suffering and knowing that He was our strength when we were weak, He was our voice when we couldn't speak,

He was our eyes when we couldn't see, He lifted us up when we couldn't reach, He gave us faith, because we believed, He's everything He is, because He loved us. It was not on our strength, but the strength and glory of Jesus Christ who returned Elijah back to us, once again. Isaiah 40:31, *"But those who hope in the Lord will renew their strength. They will soar on wings like eagles; they will run and not grow weary; they will walk and not be faint"* (NIV).

Every Milestone

We learned to live every day with no expectations. I say this because with children, there are necessary expectations. We have had to train our eyes and our hearts to not look at other children and want Elijah to be developing as they were: walking, talking, sitting up, rolling over, crawling; and other milestones that a parent excitedly waits for their child to go through. This took time for us to see Elijah as who he was; Elijah. Every milestone we hit, we celebrated and thanked Jesus for it, once again restoring hope. Eventually you realize that every moment we have is a gift, one which we could have lost many times over. How thankful we are to have every day. Matthew 6:34, *"Therefore do not worry about tomorrow, for tomorrow will worry about itself. Each day has enough trouble of its own"* (NIV).

For the next few years we were very fortunate to go through life with minor bumps and bruises. We felt that we were over the biggest obstacles in his life. Any mother of boys knows that something as minor as a scraped knee can cause concern. As moms, we just want our little boys to be safe.

Cerebral Palsy

Elijah had turned three and he still lacked muscle tone which would cause him to sometimes trip over his own feet, or lose control of his legs. Our concern led us to question his neurologist as to whether we were facing another challenge that could affect Elijah's quality of life. Unfortunately, the answer was yes, we were.

At age three, Elijah was diagnosed with cerebral palsy, which meant his condition would not get better or worse. He would be able to live a functional life, but with challenges. The doctor recommended Elijah to be fit with braces for his legs so he would have more stability to walk without falling. Over time, these braces helped him walk confidently and he could focus on gaining strength in the areas where he lacked strength, which were his legs. Packed away with his childhood memories, we still have those tiny braces. We keep them as a reminder to show him how brave and strong he was, and still is, and how faith and hope continue to bring us through the unexpected.

Because Jacob was ten years older than Elijah, he became his brother's safety net. He was so good, kind, patient, and protective of Elijah. His unconditional love for his baby brother made Rick and I so very proud.

Epilepsy

It was an early morning and I had just gotten Jacob on the bus and off to school. I was in the master bedroom making the bed when I looked over at Elijah. He was jerking his head back and forth and fluid was coming from his mouth. I immediately ran to him, picked him up and called my in-laws for help. Rick and I were fortunate to have both sets of parents living close by; my parents were just five minutes away, and Rick's parents were right next door. I called my in-laws and my father-in-law rushed over to drive us to the hospital. My mind went directly to infantile spasms, but these seemed to have a different effect on his body. He was doing things I had never seen before. As soon as the doctor examined him, we were told that it was a simple ear infection. The diagnosis seemed so simple, yet harmful. Because of all that Elijah had been through, he had a very high tolerance to pain. Often when he was in pain, it was impossible to tell. He was too young to tell us he was hurting so he just endured the day whether or not he was in pain. Seizures are very scary. One minute you will see your child appear fine and the next, convulsing or just zoning out.

After his first seizure, we started to see more of what they call atypical absence seizures. Elijah would be in a room and then suddenly, zone out and it would take him quite a while to come back to. When he would come out of the seizure, his mood would change from a happy child to a very aggressive, tired child.

Over the years these seizures continued to get worse. He was now diagnosed with epilepsy. We would be in and out of hospitals, what seemed like every other month because of anti-seizure meds. The doctor would try Elijah on a medicine and then in a month or two, we would experience more setbacks, and then we would go through a time when the medicine was working or the medicine was too strong. We seemed to be playing a game of trial and error that was anything but fun.

Special Needs – Our Two Worlds

The days dragged on and we simply took each year as it came. We learned so many lessons from having a child with special needs. There is one that I have learned to carry out throughout my lifetime... "View the world you live in and smile." Do this and you'll start to see things you've never noticed before.

Yellow Bus in our Driveway

I never really took notice of the little yellow buses on the road and here I was, looking at one in my own driveway. As I walked Elijah onto the bus, I noticed a beautiful boy who was stationed in a wheelchair. This little boy couldn't see; couldn't speak; couldn't move...yet, had a smile on his face. At that moment, I began to realize that no matter what you're dealt with, you set out in life with a smile. This moment opened our eyes to this little boy's world. A world we wanted to know more about; a world we came to know because of our child Elijah.

Diagnosis of Autism Spectrum Disorder

It seems that every time we entered a doctor's office another diagnosis was added to the list. There were times Elijah would show certain behaviors that we questioned because they were behaviors that were sensory related. After observing him for some time, the diagnosis ASD, (autism spectrum disorder) surfaced. At the time, we had no idea what autism was so we learned everything we could on how to make his world, and ours, less stressful. Elijah has sensory issues where loud noises and large crowds make him uncomfortable.

We still have very trying days and are learning everyday new techniques to overcome the obstacles associated with ASD. It has its challenges, but we adjust as best as we can. We cry, laugh, learn, and trust Jesus. He is the only one who knows Elijah and what he needs as he is forced to face these challenges in his life, one day at a time, and we continue to learn and grow together as a family.

A "Monster-Jam Truck" World

With the diagnosis of epilepsy, Elijah had to go through a time in which the doctor would manipulate his medications in an attempt to find the best prescription for preventing the seizures. This required many hospital visits and he had to be admitted each time they put him on a new medication. One medication would work for a while and just when we thought it was working something unexpected would happen and we would be right back in the hospital trying to find the right medication once again. During this time, Elijah grew very fond of Monster Jam trucks. He received his very first truck the first time he had his blood drawn to check blood levels with the medicine. If ever there was a time I could say we dreaded, it had to be when he needed to get his blood drawn.

It is so hard to hear your child crying in agony knowing there is nothing you can do about it but pray that they get the poke on the first try. Sadly, there were multiple times that they were not able to draw on the first attempt. We told Elijah that because he was a brave boy he would be able to pick out a small toy from the store as a reward for his bravery. After our appointment we went directly to the store and, of course, Elijah chose a die-cast Monster Jam Truck. Since then, Monster Jam trucks have become not only a hobby or collection, but a near obsession.

Everything was centered on Monster Jam trucks. Elijah's world was and still is today "A Monster Jam World." Every year, since the time he turned seven, Elijah's highlight of the New Year is to attend a Monster Jam Show in Detroit, Michigan with his Dad. This would become an annual father and son outing. After hearing about every exciting moment of the show it has evolved into a family tradition including Grandpa Eaton, Jacob, nephews, cousins, and Uncle Dave.

Daily routines with Elijah were quite draining. We would have to make up stories about Monster Jam trucks to get him to go to bed. He would even take them to bed with him. In the morning, Elijah did not like to brush his teeth, so I would act like I was talking to a Monster Jam truck telling it that now it was time for Monster Mutt (just one of the many names) to brush its teeth, and then would take the toothbrush and act like I was brushing its teeth raking the brush along its grill. For breakfast Monster Jam trucks had to watch him eat. Since these trucks had become such a part of everyday life, I took it a step further, to my advantage, and told Elijah that my back was a track and he could run his trucks on it. It worked every time. He was having fun and mom was getting her massage.

Monster Jam trucks go everywhere with Elijah, even to school. His teacher, Ms. Sessink, and his aide, Ms. Ashmore, came up with a clever idea on how to let me know whether Elijah had a good day at school. Every morning, Elijah would pick out a Monster Jam truck to take to school with him. It must stay in his backpack until it is time to go home. If his day was successful, meaning homework was complete, and no misbehavior, Ms. Ashmore would take a "selfie" of Elijah and his Monster Jam truck. It was a great incentive, and I enjoyed receiving a picture and the joy of Elijah when he would come home with a smile and say, "It was a great day!" Thank you, Erica and Sharon, what a wonderful idea!

Today he has collected well over 700 die-cast Monster Jam trucks and still counting. I never thought I could be so thankful for a toy, but I am so grateful for the joy they have brought my son. When we look at this collection we are reminded of all the trials he has had to endure and all the victories as well. Monster Jam trucks have become part of our family and have helped us through some of the most difficult times.

Video EEG

Elijah was still experiencing multiple seizures a day. Each year we noticed his seizure activity was affecting his quality of life. These seizures were taking a toll on him and our family. They disrupted daily life and were exhausting. After a seizure, he would forget everything he had learned at school, and we would have to start all over again. It was such a vicious cycle. All I wanted was for Elijah to live a normal life. In 2010 we found ourselves in the hospital once again. The doctors wanted to video tape him having a seizure so they could identify any abnormalities. We had been at the hospital for quite some time and Elijah did not have another seizure so the doctor took him off his anti-seizure medication in hopes it would help prompt a seizure so that they could evaluate their next steps. Once they got a good video, we could finally go home.

There were two medical interns beside Elijah's bed and I noticed that Elijah did not look well. I expressed this to the two interns who assured me that he was fine. Once again, we found ourselves unexpectedly facing another Glorified Un-Expectation; this time feeling hopeless as we knelt beside our son's bedside in the hospital. Suddenly we heard the sirens and the loud speaker blurted, "Code blue, room 7." This was Elijah's room! When you hear the words "Code Blue," it means there is a life or death situation. The patient has stopped breathing and needs to be resuscitated immediately. One minute my son was okay, and the next he's fighting for his life. The next thing I knew, the doctors were working on Elijah trying to revive him. The doctors told everyone to get out of the room. As Rick was pushed out of the room he shouted, "Elijah, don't leave me." I dropped to my knees as all my strength was gone, and was pleading with Jesus, begging him saying, "Please don't take my son. Please help us!" We knew at that moment, we needed Jesus now more than ever.

On bended knee right there in the middle of the doorway to his room, I happened to raise my head and slightly turn it to the right staring down the long hallway. Through the tears in my eyes I noticed a woman I had seen before walking towards me. It wasn't clear where I had seen her, but as she approached, I knew immediately who she was. It was the same chaplain, Cindy Howard, that had prayed with me a year earlier as I was about to give birth to my daughter. It was the same hospital, but a different room and a different floor. She put her hand on my shoulder and asked if she could pray with me. We prayed and then we heard, "We have a pulse. Get him to ICU now!" Jesus gave Elijah back to us once again, but he was seizing uncontrollably. We only knew he was breathing. We did not know if there would be any complications from lack of oxygen. Elijah had no heartbeat for two minutes.

As I look back and recall the events that took place that day, I am in awe of Jesus as He sent Chaplain Cindy Howard to us once again offering prayer and comfort as we faced the possibility of losing our beloved Elijah. Jesus, through His Mercy and His grace, gave Elijah back to us a third time. Hebrews 4:16, *"Let us then approach God's throne of grace with confidence, so that we may receive mercy and find grace to help us in our time of need"* (NIV).

Another Brain Surgery

Elijah remained in ICU for two days, seizing on and off until finally the seizures stopped. They were then able to perform tests which told us that miraculously, no permanent damage had been done. We were so thankful. Unfortunately, they were not able to get a video of any seizure activity which would allow them to better identify the contributing factors. After meeting with the doctors, they told us that the anti-seizure meds can only do so much. If Elijah's seizure disorder continued to decline, we would possibly be facing surgery to repair the damage to his brain that was causing the seizures. This was serious now. Rick and I had no answers, and just hearing the words brain surgery again was enough to make us feel defeated.

After we were stable again and on our way to recovery from that frightening experience in the hospital, we had to move fast and pray that Jesus would lead us and help us find the best facility that specializes in difficult epileptic surgeries. For two years, we would go through an observing phase where it would involve many doctor visits to the Cleveland Clinic. For a while it felt like another home away from home. Elijah's case was brought before a team of thirty professional physicians who would decide what therapy or care would most benefit Elijah. As the professional team considered whether Elijah was a candidate for epileptic surgery we waited, prayed, and anxiously awaited the phone call that would finally offer some relief for my beloved son.

Final Confirmation

I was picking up Elijah from school one day and as he sat down, I looked over at him and he was starting to drool, then suddenly went limp. I got out of my car and rushed over to the passenger's seat. As I looked around for help, all I could see was an empty parking lot. Everyone from school had left. Farther down the parking lot, I saw one van remaining. I ran to the woman behind the wheel screaming for help. The woman was a trained paramedic and once again we thanked Jesus for providing us yet another miracle. After she revived him, I immediately drove him to the ER. Once we were discharged, we waited for confirmation from the Lord as we continued to pray that Elijah would be a good candidate for epileptic surgery.

We did not get our answer right away. We continued to work with the Cleveland Clinic who performed more and more tests. Once we had results from these tests, the doctors would come together and discuss the type of brain surgery that would be most beneficial. Thankfully, the tests had helped the doctors locate and understand where the seizures were occurring. Meanwhile, Elijah continued to have seizures daily increasing our anxiety and prompting more prayer.

Finally, on Friday, February 17, 2012 we learned that Elijah had been approved for pediatric epilepsy surgery which would be performed on Thursday, March 29th. The operation would give Elijah a 70% chance of being seizure free without the need for medications. We were pleased that Dr. Bingaman, known as one of the best surgeons for this procedure would be doing the operation. We were even more relieved to learn that Dr. Bingaman had performed many of these surgeries without even one fatality. However, the best thing we were pleased to learn about the doctor is that he loves the Lord and lives in obedience to God's Word as we read in 1 Peter 4:10, *"God has given each of you a gift from his great variety of spiritual gifts. Use them well to serve one another"* (NLT). Dr. Bingaman gives Jesus the honor and credit for allowing him to perform this delicate and complicated surgery. We believed that Elijah was in the best hands humanly possible.

We were expected to be in the Cleveland Clinic for about two weeks. Elijah would be in surgery for approximately 6 – 8 hours and a nurse would update us on his progress every hour. I informed my friends and family of the details of the procedure and asked for prayer.

I started writing a daily journal at this time, noting all that we experienced up to, during, and after his surgery. Every day brought more unexpected complications along with many answered prayers and praises. You can read the full journal at the end of the book in the section entitled, "A New Beginning; Through it All." I hope you will take the time to read it as it illustrates all that we had to go through during this very stressful time and how time and again, Jesus brought us through it.

Elijah's Condition Today

It's been five years and I thank Jesus every day that Elijah has been seizure free since the surgery in 2012. Our last EEG still shows mild activity but we control it with anti-seizure medications. It is likely that Elijah will have to take this medicine for the rest of his life. Over the years, he has adjusted very well from having no left peripheral vision. He is in 10th grade and wants to continue to follow in his dad's footsteps and become a farmer. We have learned to take one day at a time; one step at time.

Having a child with special needs is trying at times. Elijah has had to experience countless medical issues. From the day he was born we have had to deal with life threatening events not to mention the diagnoses of possible cancer, brain surgeries, staph infections, vision loss, infantile spasms, cerebral palsy, epilepsy, and autism spectrum disorder. Sometimes I feel like Elijah has seen more hospitals than some doctors have! But with every battle, we have learned to place our hope in Jesus. We learned early on in his lifetime that the difficulties in his life are completely out of our control. At times, hope is all we had, yet our loving Lord Jesus has never let us down.

The bible tells us that we have much to hope for. I often lean on the scripture from Jeremiah 29:11 which states, *"For I know the plans I have for you declares the Lord, plans to prosper you and not to harm you, plans to give you a hope and a future"* (NIV). Every day we hope that Elijah's next day will be better than the last. Today we continue to follow Romans verse 12:12 which tells us, *"Be joyful in hope, patient in affliction, faithful in prayer"* (NIV). We never know what each hour, day, week, month or even year will bring, but the Lord has shown us that we do not have to fear. We simply must be hopeful, patient, and have faith.

Our human spirit sometimes gets in the way, but we can be easily reminded by imprinting on our hearts Romans 15:13 which instructs us, *"May the God of hope fill you with all joy and peace in believing, so that by the power of the Holy Spirit you may abound in hope"* (ESV). Without Christ we simply have no joy or peace. It is through faith and hope in Him that we find it. With the many difficulties in my life, and I suspect yours as well, it would be easy to become discouraged and depressed. Life does not always turn out the way we think it should. But again, we can turn to scripture knowing that God's plan is perfect. We may make a mess out of our lives, but He can take the broken pieces and still do good as we are told in Genesis 50:20 which states, *"You intended to harm me, but God intended it for good to accomplish what is now being done"* (NIV).

Anyone who has had the privilege of being a parent knows that there is no greater love. I believe that parenthood is an excellent way for Christ to show His love for us. Can you imagine sacrificing your child for a world of strangers? People who may never know you and some of those who do blatantly turn their backs on you? Yet this is what our heavenly Father did for us. *"For He so loved the world that He gave His one and only Son, that whoever believes in Him should not perish but have eternal life"* (John 3:16, NIV). This is powerful. I know that no matter what happens to my loved ones, that should they come to know Christ, I will have the opportunity to live eternally with them.

There were many times that we nearly lost Elijah. Some might say it would have been easier had Jesus taken him home early on. I resolutely disagree. Elijah has brought me and my family great joy over the years and the time we have spent with him is priceless. I can't imagine losing him and I know God has great plans for his life just as anyone else's. But I can tell you what losing a baby feels like. Let me tell you about Jaelynn.

KERRI GENE DANIELS

LOVE

Jaelynn's Story

Nothing teaches the love of Christ more than having a child and becoming a parent. Examining John 3:16 we learn that, *"For God so loved the world that He gave His one and only Son, that whoever believes in Him shall not perish but have eternal life"* (NIV). This is one of the most quoted bible verses of all time and for good reason. This verse clearly illustrates the sacrifice that God made so that we would not be doomed to eternal damnation, but have everlasting life in Him. Let me say it again, He sacrificed His Son, for us. As parents, we love our children as God loved Christ.

Anyone who has had the incredible and miraculous opportunity of holding their newborn can't help but be filled with a love like no other. It is a deep love, one that teaches us that our own sacrifice is not really a sacrifice at all. We would do anything for our children to ensure that they are safe, happy, and healthy. We sacrifice our time, our talents, and our money to ensure that they are properly taken care of. The birth of a child is nothing short of a miracle. Though we give birth to these children, we must remember that these are His children whom He has given us the gift of raising for Him. Children bring with them promise and hope - and love.

Jacob was my faith baby. Through him I learned about faith in trusting Jesus for a better future for both he and I. Together we believed Jesus would provide a daddy to come into our lives that would become a great and strong leader. He did not disappoint with the arrival of Rick into our lives. Elijah taught us about hope. The difficulties of bringing him into this world and keeping him happy, healthy, and safe have certainly been challenging. At times it was purely our hope in Christ that got us through those trying times. Our ever-growing faith and hope led Rick and I to want to bring yet another child into our family and decided to once again become pregnant.

Knowing this would be a high-risk pregnancy because of the difficulties in my past, we relied upon the faith and hope that we had learned through Jacob and Elijah. He brought us through tough times before and we were confident that with Him by our side, we would, once more, be victorious. We were willing to make whatever sacrifices necessary to bring this little girl into the world. We prayed that she would be born healthy and that any medical difficulties would be short lived. However, we must also be reminded that our plans are not always that of our Father.

When God took baby Jaelynn home so soon after her birth, we were perplexed. It was such a painful experience, one that no parent ever wants to experience. But as Proverbs 3:5 tells us we are to, *"Trust in the Lord with all your heart and lean not on your own understanding"* (NIV). God's reasons are not our reasons and it is not our place to question them, but to accept them. Our human selves find this excruciatingly difficult. Yet I can say that I am grateful that though I only had eleven minutes with her, they were eleven of the most glorious minutes of my life and they have left a love that will never end.

It is said that it is better to have love and lost than never loved at all. As difficult as it is to lose a child, I must admit that this statement is very true for me. Jaelynn will be a part of my daily life simply because God allowed it. I think of her every day and the love I have for her grows in her absence. She will always be an active part of our family. We have her memorial tree which reminds us of her and the memories of holding her tiny little body in my arms. I am so grateful that God gave her to us, for she has taught us so much about love and the love Christ has for us. It has also taught us to not take anything for granted; each moment of everyday is a gift. This is Jaelynn's story.

It's a Girl

In the fall of 2008, we received the very exciting news that would add some variety to our toy collection. Instead of tripping over hard monster trucks, tractors, and cars, our landings would be much softer with baby dolls, Barbie's, and dress ups. We were pregnant again and could not have been happier. Because of the risks we encountered with Elijah, we took measures to find the best doctor that specializes in high risk pregnancy. We found a doctor in Oregon, Ohio who had a ninety-nine percent success rate of delivering high-risk pregnancies and instantly knew this was the doctor for our baby girl.

Jaelynn's Name

We chose her name when we found out we were having a girl at 20 weeks. We named her Jaelynn Gene Daniels. We spelled her name J.A.E.L.Y.N.N. Her name is special because the "J" stands for the first letter in her big brother's name, Jacob; "A" which stands for "and," "E" stands for her other big brother Elijah; and the last part of the name, Lynn which is my husband's and father-in-law's middle name. Jaelynn's middle name, Gene, is my father's, my twin sister, and my middle name.

Because this was a high-risk pregnancy I visited the doctor every two weeks so that they could monitor my blood-pressure, check for complications such as toxemia and other factors that could be risky. Despite the risks, we were filled with joy in anticipation of our baby's arrival. I enjoyed seeing my belly grow each day. It was a reassurance that everything was going well and that in just a short time we would get to hold our baby girl. It was God's plan to give my husband a daughter, and to give her brothers a sister to love and protect. I remember going home after that appointment and walking into what would become her nursery and praying to Jesus, "Please Lord, please let me experience the joy of having no complications; to enjoy this pregnancy and not fear what could happen." As I smiled, I pictured how this room was going to turn into a beautiful elegant nursery. Oh, the fun times of planning and preparing.

Doctor's Concern – Bed Rest

At our 5 ½ month checkup, I wanted Jacob and Elijah to go with us to our next appointment so that they could experience their baby sister's heartbeat and make this a family memory. However, for this appointment I felt God telling me that this was an appointment only for me and Rick. As the doctor came in, he sat down, picked up the wand and started moving it around my belly. Minutes went by as he searched for her heartbeat. I believe that as mothers we go through a phase of "what ifs." What if he can't find it? What if something happened? One minute, two minutes, and finally there it was, the whoosh, whoosh, whoosh, of her heartbeat.

We smiled joyfully, but the doctors face showed concern. As he spoke the words, "She is very tiny" I thought to myself, well, yes, she's tiny, but still growing, right? As he looked at us, the look on his face told me that my pregnancy may not be included in his ratings of successful deliveries. Could I possibly be that one percent? Jaelynn was not developing as quickly as she should, and the blood flow was restricted. This would result in strict bed rest for me which would allow better blood flow to Jaelynn. All I could do was just hold my belly and tell her that God was with us, that He was protecting her. We were going to get through this. "You, my baby girl, are going to be just fine" I would tell her. I do not know if the tears that were falling were happy tears or tears of the unknown. I knew that we were going to be just fine.

It was not easy to lie still for twenty-four hours a day. The only time I could get out of bed was to go to the bathroom just like my pregnancy with Elijah. It really didn't bother me though. I knew that after all this was over, the best was yet to come. Our family and friends were there to help around the house and tend to meals. They lifted my spirits with prayers, visits, cards, and gifts. The bed rest and lying on my side seemed to be doing its job. She was starting to show great strides and our hope for a normal delivery grew.

Admitted to Hospital until Delivery

The excitement was cut short as another two weeks past and we were at our next doctor's appointment. The Dr. was even more concerned and told us that his best advice for us was to have another specialist involved and to be admitted into the hospital for the next three months until delivery. Jaelynn was still not growing as she should and it would be best to be close to the hospital in case we experienced meeting our daughter sooner than expected.

As we arrived at the hospital where she would be delivered, we entered the room that would become my temporary home for the next three months. A miraculous inspiration took place that day. As I looked at the bracelet on my arm; the ones they provide upon being admitted to the hospital, I noticed the numbers 3:16. I turned to my husband joyfully and said, "Oh look, this hospital must be a believing hospital because they have the verse John 3:16." Without ruining the moment, my husband graciously said, "Kerri, that's the date, March

16th, 2009." Amazing! God provided a beautiful moment at my time of need. God is so good.

High School Graduation

During my bedrest, I was planning for yet another beginning; Jacob would be graduating high school near the time of Jaelynn's delivery. As I was preparing to bring another child into the world, I was about to send another off. Since I was unable to do much, my mom and sister planned the festivities. It was a very emotional time for me. I was about to bring another baby into our lives while preparing to send my oldest off to college. It was bittersweet.

The Specialist

While in the hospital, the specialist presented us with a few options. I was not ready to hear the words that came out of his mouth. That he even would suggest abortion was enough for me to stand up, grab my belongings and with my heart filled with grief shout, absolutely not! We will do whatever we can to bring Jaelynn into this world.

Room Visitors

The days passed and one day as I was laying in my room holding my belly and feeling the kicks from a very strong little girl, I looked up and standing in the doorway was my very good friend, Starla Fick and her mother-in law. Rick could not be with me all the time because he had to work, take care of the home, and look after the boys. Knowing that, Starla would spend every extra moment she had right by my side.

The Gift of Song – Healer

Another friend, Laura Berry, was returning from a worship conference and stopped by to see me on her way home to drop off a gift she had gotten me while at the conference. It was a CD of a new Christian musician by the name of Kari Jobe who had recently released her first album. Laura knows how much I love music, so the gift was very meaningful to me. She handed it to me and I immediately put it in the CD player to listen. Wow! It was like having a church service right there in my hospital room. Kari Jobe instantly became one of my favorite Christian artists. There was one song called "Healer" that was very powerful. The lyrics of the song where exactly what my baby girl and I needed to hear. "I believe you're my Healer, I believe You're more than enough for me, Jesus You're all I need."

Yes! Jesus. You are our healer and we are going to be just fine. Then I heard the bridge, "Nothing is impossible for You, You hold my world in Your hands." It took everything I had not to get out of that bed and start moving to this amazing song. I held my belly and told Jaelynn that Jesus is our Healer. Immediately she would kick and move. Oh, the joy and memories we were making and she hadn't even entered the world yet.

As Laura was leaving we said our goodbyes and I thanked her for sharing this intimate moment with my daughter and me. We played the song repeatedly. I had never felt her kick as strong as she did when this song was played. How special that my baby girl and I already shared the same gratitude for music, and what a gift it is.

The Chaplain

Walking passed my room was Chaplain Cindy Howard. She heard the song playing and stopped to inquire as to the name and artist of the song. I shared with her and she stated that she could not wait to purchase the CD. She asked me how I was doing and I shared with her that we were doing great, that Jesus is our healer, and nothing is impossible with Him. She agreed and asked if she could pray for us. As I lowered the music and bowed my head, I once again held my belly and thanked Jesus for this precious life that I would soon meet. I anticipated holding her in my arms, praising and worshiping our Heavenly Father. As we prayed, strength that I could not even describe filled my soul and I was ready to face this moment with faith, hope, and strength as my weapons...a smile included.

As I lay in my hospital bed I began thanking God for new beginnings. It was March and spring was just around the corner. I have always loved spring because it's that time when the flowers and plants are waking up from their cold winter slumber. Soon new life would begin and soon we would be blessed with a new life all our own.

Better Chances

Every morning we were scheduled for an ultrasound to help the doctors decide whether Jaelynn's blood flow was increasing or decreasing. Unfortunately, it was decreasing and a chill traveled up my spine. I then heard the doctors exclaim, "We need to deliver now! Jaelynn would have a better chance outside the womb than inside." We had heard this before and we were ready. We were ready because we had already experienced the unexpected of the NICU. We knew that if we could go through it with Elijah, then we could go through it with Jaelynn as well.

Jaelynn is Born

On March 20, 2009, at 6:28 pm the first day of spring, we gave birth to a tiny baby girl. She was so beautiful. She had my hair, my dimples in her cheeks, and daddy's little dimple in her chin. We did it. She's here. Jesus, nothing is impossible for you. Thank you. I looked up at my husband and just knew he was thinking the same thing that I was...Let the rollercoaster ride begin, only this time the ride would end much sooner than expected. As we watched the doctor bring her tiny body over to us, and gently lay her in my arms, he sincerely spoke the words, "I'm sorry. She is too tiny for our equipment. You can have as much time as you need with your daughter."

Time stood still. For eleven minutes we held our baby girl, cheek to cheek. We were very thankful for the time we had with her and the few precious memories that we made with our little girl right there in that operating room. I will never forget seeing her proud daddy holding her. We both looked at her and told her she would soon be in the arms of Jesus who brought us so much faith, hope and love. She let out a sweet little cry of assurance and with a little smile all her own, passed away peacefully. At that moment, Jesus, her Healer, had received His first little flower of spring.

Surgery Complications

As we were giving her to Jesus, the surgeon told Rick he had to leave the room. I was losing too much blood and would have to go into surgery immediately. Time was non-existent and I continued to deny that my baby girl was gone. I continued to plead with the nurse insisting that my baby was fine. All I could hear was the countdown, ten, nine, eight, seven...I then fall into a deep sleep. Two beautiful things happened while I was under. Our family was able to remain in the room where Jaelynn was delivered while I was whisked off to surgery. There they were able to see and hold her for the last time. Also, I experienced a glorified unexpected vision.

A Beautiful Vision

As I succumbed to the anesthesia, I closed my eyes and was taken to a beautiful pasture with the bluest skies I've ever seen. I saw a tree in the far distance. As I looked out into the opened beautiful site, I could see her. She's not a baby. Her brownish-blonde hair is blowing as she runs away from me. I could not see her face, but I felt unbelievable joy as I stay stationed watching her run, waving her hand, as in waving goodbye for now, and as I'm smiling, I raised my hand and waved back to her.

Reality Hits Home

I open my eyes and I'm in a dark room lying in a hospital bed. Beside me was my baby girl resting in her bedside crib dressed in her white gown. I see my husband, and my friends, Starla and Laura sitting beside me with a look of sorrow. I had gone into shock and still believed that my baby girl was with me. The nurse brought her to me and reminded me that during the delivery we had lost her and that I had been in surgery for four hours due to complications. Her little arm twitched and I remember exclaiming, "She's alive." Again, I saw nothing but concerned looks. It's true? My baby died? I was so confused. In my mind, I was prepared and ready for the NICU. We even had a room waiting for us. I remember just wanting to hold her. The nurse walked over gently picking her up and laid her in my arms. I looked at her and knew she was not there. Her body was, but she wasn't. The vision of her as a little girl running to her Jesus is what I wanted to hold on to.

Friends Holding Jaelynn

Starla and Laura were beside me, and each one took turns holding her. I will never forget those moments and how these two special sisters in Christ never left my side. I know it was after midnight and they were there most of the night until I could regain my composure.

Visit from Tiny Purpose

The following day, Alaina Hiatt, co-founder of Tiny Purpose, came and offered her condolences, brought us a memorial box of the most meaningful gifts to remember our baby, and offered her assistance anytime needed. Alaina shared with me her own heart-wrenching un-expectation of losing a baby, her daughter, Hope Elizabeth. Tiny Purpose exists in the hope of being able to help grieving mothers understand that their baby's too-short life has a purpose – a purpose extending into eternity. They desire to be a place where women can grieve, grow and heal; and a place where they have the opportunity to help other mothers, in turn fulfilling the Lord's eternal purpose. She could relate to the emptiness you feel when someone, a part of you, has died. Thank you, Starla and Laura, for your friendship and sharing the most meaningful memory of my life, and Alaina for your friendship, and offering support to other mothers who experience the loss of a child. I will never forget the love they provided.

The Love and Help of those around Me

Losing a child is one of the most devastating things a parent can experience. However, in my time of need, I had a variety of people rally around me. First my father-in-law offered to have Jaelynn's body released to him so that he could personally drive her to Anderson's Funeral Home who graciously provided their services for no charge. My twin sister Sherri, created a video of the moments we had with Jaelynn in the operating room, and my mother crocheted a beautiful pink baby blanket that we placed in her casket along with a family photo. Mom Daniels sewed a beautiful lace skirt with baby roses to wrap around her casket and Starla had Jaelynn's baby blanket engraved with Jaelynn's name and her birthdate. Finally, Aunt Sue Bockrath created a delightful scrapbook with pictures of Jaelynn.

Jaelynn's Celebration Service – Salvation Message

Jaelynn's celebration service was special because the pastor, Scott Winsted of Crossroads Community Church, spoke about the gift of life and how salvation is available to everyone who believes in Jesus Christ. Scott has such a way of bringing the bible to life by sharing the words of Jesus. As Scott delivered the message, people were brought to know that same kind of love; the love of Jesus Christ. Laura Berry opened the service with her beautiful voice as she sang, "How Great is Our God" and "Amazing Grace My Chains Are Gone" by Chris Tomlin. Pete Bishop played the piano. I am so thankful for these wonderful people in my life that contributed to making her celebration service as special as it was because it was all for the glory of Jesus Christ.

Jaelynn's Service – Elderly Woman

As everyone was in line waiting to say their respects to Rick and me, I was sitting next to Jaelynn's casket because it had only been a few days since the C-section. I was feeling the pain not just emotionally, but physically. An elderly woman approached me, leaned down and whispered in my ear, "Don't worry honey, Jesus is coming soon." I did not recognize this woman and looked up at Rick. I mouthed the words,

"Who was that? Do you know her?" and he said, "no." That was all she said and then she was gone.

Jaelynn's Service – Healer Song

At the closing of her celebration service, Rick and I thought it would be fitting to play the song that she and I shared in the hospital; the song, "Healer." We wanted everyone to know that no matter what answer you receive from your prayers, we rejoice because He is our Healer. Here on Earth and in heaven above because his Word claims, when we die, we live. Romans 14:8, *"If we live, we live for the Lord; and if we die, we die for the Lord. So, whether we live or die, we belong to the Lord"* (NIV). She is alive with Christ in heaven, and what greater joy knowing that we have a daughter who stands in the presence of Jesus. He will give us what we need to overcome the pain of all the unknown memories, the birthdays that will pass, and the deep understanding without her in our arms. I go back to when she was safe in my womb and the movement and strength I felt from her as "Healer" was playing. I hold on to that beautiful moment, because that was a moment we shared, worshiping our Jesus together.

Memorial Tree Gift

We received so many beautiful flower arrangements and gifts. One of the gifts we received was a flowering tree to be planted in memory of Jaelynn. We wanted to plant it where we would be able to see it anywhere from looking out our back windows. We found the perfect spot right in the center of our back yard. This gift meant so much to us because it was alive and we would be able to watch it grow representing how old she would be if she was here celebrating life with us.

The Bright Blue Bird

On May 7, 2009, two months after laying Jaelynn to rest, we celebrated the first Mother's Day without her. I was sitting at the kitchen table crying and just feeling so confused and lost without her. I looked out the sliding glass doors, and there in the backyard, I noticed that her tiny tree had grown to look like a cross. It was so green and alive, and on one of the branches a pink flower had bloomed. I was so thankful for this moment because I knew Jesus knew the pain I was experiencing. I believe that He knew I would notice that little pink flower and be reminded that He had received His first flower of spring. Right before my eyes, I saw the most beautiful bright bluebird land on top of her tree. It was a species I had never seen before. My sorrow instantly turned to joy after experiencing this moment. Psalm 126:5, *"Those who sow with tears will reap with songs of joy"* (NIV).

Mother's Day Surprise

Later that day we were getting ready to leave to celebrate Mother's Day with our family and I asked Rick if we could go to K-mart to get our mothers hanging flower baskets. We are walking the center aisle, and as I looked up, I see her walk past us. It was the mysterious elderly woman at the funeral home who spoke to me telling me not to worry, Jesus is coming soon. I looked at Rick and told him I had to go talk to her. It was just a few seconds, and as I turned around, and looked back, she was nowhere to be found. I believe in my spirit Jesus placed her there to remind me of what she said at Jaelynn's funeral "Don't worry honey, Jesus is coming soon." Revelation 22:20, *"He who testifies to these things says, "Yes, I am coming soon." Amen. Come, Lord Jesus"* (NIV). He knew that this day would be very difficult so he sent her for comfort.

Meaning of a Name

It was June 2009 and again, I was sitting at the kitchen table when Elijah asked me a question that had never entered my thoughts. He wanted to know the meaning behind Jaelynn's name. My response to him was I did not know if it had a meaning as we created the name using symbolism from our families' names. I was curious if it really did have a meaning so I went to the computer and typed her name in the search box. I was not exactly prepared for what I was about to read. A black screen popped up with the words "Girl" highlighted and it reads, "CRESTED BLUEBIRD." Elijah is waiting for me to say something, but instead he sees another day of tears streaming down my face, and a look as if I had seen something unbelievable. I had to do a double-take; I had just witnessed another Glorified Un-Expectation. My mind wandered back to the morning on Mother's Day, where just last month, I took a picture of a blue bird sitting on top of her memorial tree.

Could that be the same type of bird that had such an impact in my soul that out of sorrow brought joy? After going back on-line and researching all types of birds, I was certain, that yes, this was a crested bluebird. The crested bluebirds are called Jaelynn's. You cannot make this up. I was so thankful for that moment because for the last three months I had felt like Jesus had left and that I was alone trying to figure out what went wrong. My thoughts and emotions were everywhere, and it felt like a part of me had died with her. I've learned to train my eyes to seek Jesus in everything.

Kari Jobe, Christian Music Artist

Once again, another Glorified Un-Expectation occurred two months after the revelation of the crested bluebird. As I put Kari Jobe's CD in to listen to the song "Healer," I picked up the sleeve of the CD, and I noticed above Kari Jobe's name was a bluebird. Once again, I am blessed with a gift that only God can provide. This was so amazing to me that I couldn't keep this silent. It was a miracle. In my eyes, it was an answer to my question, as I cried out to Him, "Jesus, where are you? Do you not see the pain I suffer? I can't do this on my own. Please help me!" The following week our story was received by an organization called National Right to Life and a reporter wrote an article about our story titled, "The Precious Life of Baby Jaelynn."

Newspaper Article
The Precious Life of Baby Jaelynn
By Liz Townsend, National Right to Life, 2009

What does Obama's Abortion Agenda mean? Pro-lifers could give many well-informed answers to that question, but it really comes down to children like

Baby Jaelynn Daniels, who was born March 20 at 29 weeks old. Jaelynn only lived for 11 short minutes, but to her parents she was perfect. That Obama would support aborting such precious babies, that he would hide their personhood in the rhetoric of choice, is an abomination to Rick and Kerri Daniels.

"I just can't imagine how a family man like Obama could do what he's trying to do," Kerri Daniels told NRL News. "When you see pictures of Jaelynn, you can see that this is actually a human life that he says can be aborted. You can see she's beautiful, with a little bit of hair. She even has my husband's dimple on her chin."

The Daniels, of Adrian, Michigan, were aware early on that the pregnancy would be difficult. They had ultrasounds taken at every doctor visit, which showed problems with blood flow to Jaelynn. Those ultrasound videos are now a comfort to the family, as they can see their baby girl's growth and development while still safe in her mother's womb.

"At 20 weeks, we got great videos of her opening her mouth," Mrs. Daniels said. "We could see her feet and hands. We were really excited."

With no improvement in blood flow, the Daniels went to a specialist. The doctor told them in no uncertain terms that their best option would be to abort the baby. "But we said absolutely not," recalled Mrs.

Daniels. "We would go through anything to give Jaelynn a chance."

Kerri Daniels went on complete bed rest and then remained in the hospital, trying to give her baby time to develop until term. The doctor who urged them to abort continued to give the same advice, while describing the difficulties that parents have with enduring their babies' stays in the neonatal intensive care unit (NICU).

But the doctor underestimated the family's faith and determination. The Daniels spent time in the NICU after the birth of their now-nine-year-old son, Elijah. He was born at 30 weeks weighing two pounds and has cerebral palsy, but the Daniels and their oldest son, Jacob, 18, consider him their "miracle baby." They were willing to spend more time there if they had to.

With Jaelynn's condition getting no better, she had to be delivered at 29 weeks. Jaelynn weighed a tiny eight ounces. The 11 minutes that her parents and oldest brother spent with her are irreplaceable and give them immense comfort in their grief.

"Oh, the things I got to tell her," Mrs. Daniels remembered. "We were able to get pictures and to hold her. She let out a little cry. And then she went home to God."

There is no doubt that the past three months have been heart-wrenching for the Daniels family. "But we know God gave her to us for a reason," Mrs. Daniels said. Jaelynn has touched even the doctor who urged abortion. "We got a letter from him saying he was sorry for the loss of our little girl," she continued. "He also said that if we wanted to try again his assistance is available."

The ultrasound videos and her pictures are clear visual proof of the humanity of Jaelynn and of other tiny, vulnerable babies. "If you're for abortion, this is what you're doing," said Mrs. Daniels. "Obama needs to know that he supports killing God's creation. If my daughter, who is resting peacefully in her Father's arms in heaven, was born to change this nation's decision about abortion and give other babies a chance, then Glory to God."

Jaelynn's Journal

I will always remember two days after Jesus carried her home, and she breathed her first breath in heaven, I went back to her journal and wrote *"He gives and takes away. May the name of the Lord be praised"* Job 1:21 (NLT). There is not a day that goes by I don't think of her. Even though she was here for a short time, the memories of holding her and telling her, sharing with her the love of Jesus, and then hearing her sweet cry of assurance, lives on until eternity when we are once again reunited. Jaelynn is alive in heaven, and although, I'm here, still in this world, His truth remains that He is preparing a place for me. Not just for me, but for everyone who accepts Jesus Christ as their personal Savior.

Broken Angel

The day before Jaelynn would have been seven, something unexpected happened. That evening, when we arrived home from my parent's house, there was a large box on the door step. It was from my sister Sherri and her husband, Manuel. I picked it up and set it on the counter and as I opened it, I see this beautiful statue of a little girl holding a bluebird. I lifted her out of the box and saw the bluebird, and was very excited. But something else caught my eye; inside the box were broken wings. It was a statue of a little girl with wings holding a bluebird. I immediately felt sad because here was this perfect gift and it was broken. I called my sister and shared the unexpected news and she said she would call the company to see if we could return it and get a new one. No more than two minutes passed and Rick proclaimed, "No, we can fix it. It will be okay." I agreed, and as I wiped the tears from my eyes, a smile came to my face because here lays a hidden message. Without the wings, she looked like a little girl. Me. She's broken.

She may break again, but can be fixed. Jesus is going to restore my brokenness and fix my soul and make me brand new. Again, only the love of Jesus could orchestrate something like that. So, with that perfect ending for the night, before Jaelynn's 7th birthday in heaven with her Jesus, and a new beginning in the morning, we glued her wings back on and just like we thought, she looked brand new. Thank You, Jesus!

Jaelynn's Memorial Tree is Dying

Jesus gave me my husband, my children, and He gave us the message of Jaelynn's memorial tree. It's a symbol and a reminder that He is alive and Jaelynn is in His presence. Three years ago, we had a hard winter with temperatures dipping into the single digits. During that winter, her tree started to die even though we couldn't see it as everything lay dormant during the long winter months. We saw few signs of life anywhere. When spring finally arrived and we began to see the beauty of life once again, we saw that part of Jaelynn's memorial tree was damaged. There was no life on one side of the tree, but the bark on the other side was turning black. However, the naked eye is not able to see what's going on beneath the surface. Just like one's soul.

No one can see your soul or what's going on inside except Jesus. When I look at Jaelynn's tree today and see one side dead, dark, no color or life, and the other side; beautiful, colorful, and full of life, I'm reminded of His message; when we die, we live, and the end is only the beginning. But because her tree remains connected to the main root, last spring Jesus brought new life by growing a new sprout, a new tree, representing new life. In addition, in yet another Glorified Un-Expectation, we get to experience the birth of new baby bluebirds.

Three years ago, if I would have said yes when Rick asked me if we should pull the tree, I would have missed the message. Something inside me told me not to pull it, and I listened to that inner voice within. Thank You, Jesus. If we stay connected to the main root, Jesus Christ we will never die. Jesus represents the root. When we accept Him as our personal Savior, we die to self, and receive a new life in Him, a new beginning just as we read in 1 Corinthians 5:17. I have had to cling tight to Jesus from the very moment I accepted Him as my Lord and Savior. He continues to teach me through the pain and suffering that His Glory is the only thing that matters. He didn't promise there would not be suffering. Why? Because He knew that without suffering, we could not grow into the likeness of Him.

I have had to learn to look beyond the suffering and focus on His promise in Hebrews 12:2, *"We must focus our eyes on Jesus, the author and finisher of our faith"* (KJ21). Our strength will grow and our characteristics will begin to mold into the likeness of Jesus Christ as He shapes us into the person He desires us to become, even if it feels uncomfortable. Isaiah 64:8 proclaims, *"Yet you, Lord, are our Father. We are the clay, you are the potter; we are all the work of your hand"* (NLT).

Grief

I did not know what real grief was until I had to say goodbye to my baby girl. Nothing can prepare you for the deep ache in your heart that physically grabs hold of you as it feels like you can't breathe. I felt so empty and lost, especially on the very first Mother's Day without her.

Supernatural Gift – Holy Spirit

Prayer never goes unheard. It's at these moments that I realize that He is doing something far greater than my eyes, heart, and soul, could comprehend. Just as Jesus said to His disciples, when He was explaining why He had to leave them, He said, *"You will be glad I go away, because then the comforter will be able to come to you."* John 16:7 (NIV). That comforter is the gift of the Holy Spirit.

The Holy Spirit is a supernatural gift that fills us to move forward when we can't take another step, or feel lost when we have nowhere to go. It's this free gift that you can't see, but you have access to if you have accepted Him as your personal savior. The other gifts He provides are through His creation. These gifts are beautiful and are seen with the naked eye; His creation. We don't praise the creation. We praise the Creator. Only Jesus could multiply His gifts and this is exactly what He did on Mother's Day and thereafter. Thank you, Jesus, for sending a crested bluebird (a Jaelynn) to remind me that You are watching over us.

Though Jaelynn's life was brief, the impact of her little life has been beyond measure. Carrying a child in one's womb creates a bond that only a mother can understand. Though she only lived for eleven minutes on this earth, we shared months of bonding as I carried her. Having been subjected to bedrest, my family had to make adjustments. I was unable to provide the support needed in running a household and taking care of Elijah's daily needs. There were days I felt so helpless and guilty that my family had to do the things I would normally do but simply could not at the time. No one ever complained because we knew the sacrifice was well worth it. After her birth, I nearly lost my own life as the pregnancy was especially brutal on my body and complications after her birth required emergency medical intervention. Again, it was all worth it in the end even though we lost her so soon after her blessed arrival. And a blessed arrival it was. God had a plan even for her short life. She touched so many people and through this book I pray that she will continue to do so.

Without Jaelynn, I would not know grief as I have experienced. It may seem strange that I could possibly be thankful for grief, but it showed me many things. First, it showed me how deeply one can truly love and how God must have grieved giving His only Son so that we may live through Him. According to Romans 3:23 we read, *"We all have sinned and fall short of the glory of God"* (NIV). Yet He still made the choice to sacrifice His one and only Son. Sacrificing Jaelynn was not my choice. In fact, I fought hard to keep her. Second, through here memorial service, it gave others the opportunity to hear the message of salvation; hopefully prompting some to truly consider the life that God has for them and His eternal gift of salvation. Finally, it has taught me how to be sympathetic to others who are struggling with the loss of a child. No one wants to have to suffer the loss of losing a loved one, specifically their own child, but unfortunately it happens.

I have learned to turn to Christ when I begin to miss her or begin to wonder "what if?" It simply was not meant to be and I have had to learn to trust that God knows why and that is enough for me. It's not easy but I know it would be impossible without Christ! We have all heard of stories of marriages breaking up after the loss of a child, or addiction, even suicide. The pain is deep, I know. But God can give us comfort when nothing else will.

I miss Jaelynn every day, in fact there is not a day that goes by that I do not think of her. I am grateful for the many reminders that God gave me throughout my pregnancy with her that help me even today. I have her memorial tree that continues to grow and is a constant reminder that God is continually renewing. I have the blue birds as reminders, the songs of Kari Jobe, and of course my "broken" angel with wings, because yes, there will be other times when we may break, but Jesus will be right there to put the pieces of our lives back together, guiding and helping us to begin again. We'll be made new, just like Jaelynn is in heaven. Jesus' promise in His Word says in Hebrews 13:8, *"He is the same yesterday, today, and forever"* (NIV), and I know that with all my heart, soul, and mind, Jaelynn is with me yesterday, today, and forever, just as we are with Jesus Christ.

The last twenty-three years have been very hard. One thing I do know, Jesus is aware of every moment because He knows the outcome and orchestrates our life's story by revealing His glory in every moment of our lives.

If there is one lesson I have learned through this time in my life, it is that Jesus provides His grace and mercy at the perfect moment. Lives are filled with challenges and complications, we experience loss and grief. These are a natural part of everyone's life; if we had known the outcome in the very beginning, we would probably do everything in our power to prevent it allowing us to escape the pain. Would Rick and I want to know the reason behind why Elijah had to go through all that pain and suffering, and the challenges he continues to face today? Would we want to know why Jesus called Jaelynn home to be with Him rather than us? No. Jesus knew every moment of our lives, knowing we would face many Glorified Un-Expectations and that we would need someone to cling to during the pain and suffering. He knew that one day we would look back and see Him in every minute of the unknown. He was working all things out for the good, if we choose to believe – like in Romans 8:28, *"And we know that God causes everything to work together for the good of those who love God and are called according to his purpose for them"* (NLT).

What we have come to learn through Glorified Un-Expectations is that we can make plans, have dreams, and set goals in our lives, but if it's not what God has already predestined for us from the very beginning it's meaningless. As we consider Ecclesiastes, our lives are not our own. They belong to the One who never left us through the moments of pain and suffering.

Writing this book has been my mountain. It has been a long, hard climb, but God continues to have me climb this mountain, hand in hand, clinging to Him, and never letting go. If I let go, what would happen? I'd fall right back to where I began. I would end up right back at rock bottom. Yes, I've fallen many times. There were days when I thought we were getting closer to the top but then my grasp on Him would loosen, He tried to catch me, but because of my choice to let go I would once again fall. I don't know exactly where we are on the mountain, but He does. But what I do know is that I haven't reached the top because I'm still here in this world. Will there be more "Glorified Un-Expectations?" Yes. I will not reach that top of the mountain until I see Jesus face to face. I would call that moving a mountain.

To move you either go forward or backward. I choose to walk forward with God being my leader. To walk by faith with Him; hand in hand, moving me up that mountain and carrying my cross, striving to reach the top. Matthew 16:24, *"Then Jesus said to his disciples, 'If any of you wants to be my follower, you must give up your own way, take up your cross, and follow me'"* (NLT). What is your mountain? What weighs the heaviest in your life? Move with that mountain. Walk with sorrow. Walk with that heavy heart. Start moving up that mountain and climb with the One who can get you to the top, Jesus Christ. With faith we press on, with hope we grasp his cloak, and with love we never let go because Jesus never lets us go.

KERRI GENE DANIELS

.

The Never Ending Story

This story began many years ago and God willing has many yet to come. Since finishing the manuscript for Glorified Un-Expectations, a variety of occurrences have taken place. I was once warned by a dear friend that once I began to really get serious about bringing this book to market, whose purpose is to glorify God, that the enemy would come at me strong and hard; and he has.

During the Christmas season of 2017, Rick and Elijah volunteered to deliver Christmas trees for a fundraiser for a local organization. With a full load on a trailer, Rick was turning onto a road when he accidentally hit a utility pole. It was a minor scrape and he was unaware that he had even hit it. However, a motorist behind him alerted authorities and he was later cited for a hit and run requiring him to appear in court in January, 2018. After all is said and done, this good deed ended up costing us not only time, but also points on his driving record and an unexpected court cost, which really is not glorified at all; an *Un*-Glorified Unexpectation.

After 5 years of being seizure free, the end of the year 2017 brought about yet another seizure for our dear Elijah. This was a shock to us and left us a bit unnerved as since his surgery we believed that seizures were a part of his past. However, here we were, once again wondering what to expect next. After taking him back to his neurologist, we found that this had possibly been a result of needing to adjust his medication. He had grown much over the last five years, maturing from a boy into a young man. His medication has been adjusted and we have not had another seizure, praise Jesus. We hope and pray that we don't, but we also know that nothing is guaranteed in this life. What we do know is that we have a loving God who is in control and we can rely on Him no matter what.

A few weeks after the seizure incident, Rick was rushed to the emergency room. He had a kidney stone that had unexpectedly blocked one of his kidneys. Within a few hours we were told Rick had acute kidney failure which resulted in having emergency surgery with a fever of 101.1 and a five-day stay in the hospital. Unfortunately, the surgeon was not able to remove the stone. We are hoping and praying that it is no longer there. Only Jesus knows that answer. There have been no flare-ups or pain, so we are very thankful.

Another situation involved Jacob who is now married with three beautiful children; Manolo, Aras and Camila. He was working as a manager in a firm that helped families who are experiencing the challenges of Autism. He loved his job and was doing well when he found that the company was participating in illegal activities and fraud. Once he discovered this and reported it to what he thought was the correct authorities, he was promptly fired. This situation has led to a bought of depression and hardship for his family. God will open a door. I know that God is with him, In fact, I believe that his firing was only the beginning for the amazing things God wants to do with his life. Jacob loves the Lord and therefore I believe that he will be successful in his new career, or whatever door God chooses to open for Jacob.

Right after Jacob lost his job, a few weeks before Christmas in 2017, we were subpoenaed by the courts with a lawsuit for another good deed. Two years ago, 2015, our son Jacob, and daughter-in-law, were staying at our house for a few days. Marisa needed to borrow the car to get to her job and upon returning home early morning; she was involved in a motor vehicle accident. No one was hurt at the time. We are now being sued by the other party involved because we are the owner of the vehicle. Not sure how the glorified part works in that, but again, Jesus knows so we will continue to put our trust in Him.

We are not strangers to adversity and we know that these challenges are no surprise to God because His promise is revealed in 1 Peter 4:12-13; "Dear friends, do not be surprised at the painful trial you are suffering as though something strange were happening to you. But rejoice that you participate in the sufferings of Christ, so that you may be overjoyed when His glory is revealed" (NIV).

We will continue to praise God as we place every "Glorified Un-Expectation" in His hands and pray that His will be done on earth as it is in heaven.

Don't be afraid of the unexpected. Rejoice, because this is where He wants you so He can teach you the next step to write your "Never Ending Story." When you are ready to climb your mountain and write your "Glorified Un-Expectations" life story for His glory, please contact me at kerridanielsministries.com. Together we can share what God is doing, giving glory, honor, and praise where it is due, to Jesus Christ our Lord, Amen.

A New Beginning

A 25 Day Journey

As we prepared for Elijah's upcoming brain surgery I made it my mission to recount what we would be going through. Below you will see a nearly day by day excerpt of our journey. As you read I pray that you will see how God's glorious grace was with us at all times. Most of the journal entries were written by me; however there were days that for whatever reason I was not able to provide the entry. Therefore, I have included the author as well as the date and time of each entry.

THROUGH IT ALL - Day 1
09:48PM EDT on Tuesday, March 20, 2012

Dear Jesus,

Thank you for such a wonderful day as we celebrated our daughter Jaelynn's birthday and I just thank you so much for Your strength and how You brought us through with another memory we can forever instill in our hearts. This morning started out rocky but my friend Stephanie came over and dragged me out of the house. I am so glad You sent her because we had such a great time. You, God amaze me every day and I love the surprises you bring us. Of all days, today, as we were driving to Jackson we were trying to find a radio station that would come in clearly when we finally found one. As we listened, we heard a story about a husband and wife who had lost their baby girl. I looked at Stephanie with my mouth wide opened in awe of what we were hearing. I kept nodding my head as the husband and wife were explaining how in every situation whether tragic or good, we give God praise because we don't know the plans He has for us, only He does and so we cry out to God saying, "Help us God," You see the bigger picture here.

Today I can say with a smile just like my daughter had when she breathed her last breath, Thank You Jesus for those 11 minutes we had with her. A parent's greatest joy is to share Jesus' love and before we said "soon you'll be in His arms," she let out a strong cry and then peacefully rested in His arms. Thank you, Jesus, for giving us those few minutes that have changed our family's life forever.

When I got home I found a box from my sister Sherri and Manuel. Inside was a beautiful ceramic angel with beautiful flowers. Thank you so much. Mom and Dad Daniels bought Jaelynn a beautiful basket of flowers and tulips we will be able to plant. We placed flowers and wrote her name on the cross at her resting place. It was so beautiful. Mom and Dad Eaton had called and left a message telling Elijah that when he goes to Jaelynn's resting place, there will be a purple bug holding a balloon, and he was to release it as he wishes her happy birthday. Mom also said that when she was in Barrett's store, the purple bug caught her attention and she couldn't pass it up. She said it was like Jaelynn was saying, "I want that, I want that" something only a child would like.

As I write this with tears coming down, happy tears, my brother-in-law David Daniels called us (they live across the street) and said, "Go out to your front porch and look over to our house" As we stepped onto the front porch we saw a light but was uncertain as to what it was. It became brighter and brighter and then suddenly, it floated up into the air. It was the most beautiful site I ever saw. It was a luminary lantern. What a wonderful memory. Thank you so much Jesus, for Uncle Dave, Aunt Katie, Korah Beth, Nathan, and Silas Daniels. This was a perfect ending for her 3rd birthday with this beautiful gift. It also served as a beautiful reminder that when it seems you're at your darkest hour the light still shines. That light is Jesus Christ. May He be your light. We'll talk to you tomorrow. We love You Jesus, Amen.

THROUGH IT ALL - Day 2
10:09PM EDT on Wednesday, March 21, 2012

Dear Jesus,

Thank you for our special family and friends who have joined us in this new beginning You have provided. Thank you friends and family for all the birthday messages on behalf of Jaelynn. Just to know our daughter's memory lives on to those who are close to us means so much.

Lord, today was a very quiet day. Elijah was sleeping, so I had a chance to go outside and just take in the beautiful weather. Thank you, Jesus for the flowers and new growth. As I walked back inside it felt, once again, very quiet. Then the thoughts came, "How can it be a quiet day when in 4 1/2 days we leave for Cleveland Clinic. There's so much to do, so much to plan...then that still voice you hear says "Now wait. You need to stop this! Go back outside and take it all in; the colors, the new growth, the blue skies." So that's what I did. Beautiful! Thank You, Jesus. So as I'm taking this all in I look down and see...you got it...weeds. Can you guess what happened next? Yep, I started pulling those babies out. Nothing wrong with getting your hands a little dirty!

Speaking of dirty, I am reminded of a funny story. Rick was at work and within a couple hours of working hard he noticed he had something on his pants. At first, not realizing what it was, he looked closer and discovered he had his farm pants on. These farm pants are soiled with everything you can think of including stains, worn out knees, holes, etc. So as soon as he noticed, he went from a usual day of work to being completely embarrassed trying to hide his stains. When he told me the story I had to laugh because sometimes life is like that.

We share this because Elijah's life right now is like he's wearing those soiled jeans, (Epilepsy). When God see's those soiled jeans he takes them and cleans them and makes them brand new again (Elijah's surgery). This is our prayer dearest Jesus that Your will be done in Elijah's life; that each stain inside his head (representing the seizures) will be removed as we trust in You by faith and we rest in Your goodness and grace. We all have stains in our lives and I thank You so much Father for sending Your son Jesus to take my sins (stains) away. I look forward to being with you tomorrow. We'll talk soon. Love You Jesus. Amen.

THROUGH IT ALL - Day 3
11:09 PM EDT on Thursday, March 22, 2012

Dear Jesus,

You amaze me every day. When I wake up and hear the birds singing and I walk out of the bedroom tired and not sure if I'm ready to start the day, all I have to do is look out the window and make a choice. Am I going to worry as the days come closer to surgery and sleep the day away because of the occasional fear I have, or am I going to step out in faith and live the words of Jesus in Exodus 33:14, *"The Lord replied, 'My Presence will go with you, and I will give you rest'"*(NIV)? Jesus, I need rest, but I think the "rest" You are talking about is different. I don't think it's to go back to bed and sleep though; sometimes that is what I feel like doing. The "rest" You're wanting me to do is to take in everything around me and to thank

God for everything. Here's a tip for those who have children: do this before your children wake up.

Thank You, God, for spring and new growth. We are so thankful for Elijah's "New Beginning" because it too, will be a time of new growth for him. Oh, how wonderful that after Elijah's surgery, he will learn and understand things more clearly. Because of Elijah's daily seizures, he forgets everything he's taught, so we can't wait to see how Your plan unfolds as we see Elijah gain new growth physically and spiritually. So God, my choice is to rest in You and look around and thank You for everything.

As I stepped outside I noticed a bluebird perched on top of our bluebird house. What a beautiful gift God, Thank You. I go back inside grab my camera and start snapping pictures. I see not one, but two. A male, and a female, and I realize they are making their nest. But as I was watching them, it reminded me of a verse I had read in Your Word the other day (Matthew 8:20*), "Jesus says, Foxes have holes and birds of the air have nests, but the Son of Man has no place to lay His Head"*(NIV). So, as I watch the bluebirds making their nests, I'm drawn to this verse and wonder why it keeps coming to mind.

How sad Jesus. You didn't have a place to lay Your head. God, I'm not sure where You're going with this. Please help me understand. I pray and ask the Holy Spirit what this means. "Foxes have holes and birds of the air have nests, but the Son of Man (Jesus) has no place to lay His head. I'm curious God, so I went inside to get my bible and started reading. I noticed that after this verse, Jesus didn't sleep much. Then I saw it. I was just skimming through the topics and toward the end of the book of John words written in red stood out. John 19:30

states, *"It is finished. With that He bowed His head and gave up His Spirit"* (NIV). Oh Jesus, now You have a place to lay Your head. Oh my! Thank You so much Father for helping me understand this by noticing these two blue birds, making their nest and guiding me to Your Word. I am so thankful to Your Son Jesus for giving up His Spirit, by dying on the cross so I can be forgiven of my sins. I get it!

Thank you, Jesus, for You know the suffering and trials of our lives, You know on Monday we leave for Cleveland. You know Your child Elijah will have surgery, not to harm him, but to protect him as You have done for me...for all of us. Because You knew You would live here on earth in human flesh so You could know our suffering, and now we can do what You did and go directly to the Father in heaven in prayer. Thank you again Jesus. Thank you because if I had chosen to go back to bed, I wouldn't have noticed the bluebirds You sent; I wouldn't have noticed that even the birds have a place to rest; and I wouldn't have chosen to search deeper for the meaning behind Your Word.

You knew everything and the pictures are a remembrance of how exciting it is to wake up to a brand-new day, and to make the right choice, to rest in You. Thank you, Jesus for Your Word, Psalm 30:5, *"Weeping may stay for a night, but rejoicing comes in the morning"* (NIV). After all You have shown me today Lord, I can't wait to spend time with You tomorrow. I am looking forward to it. I love You Jesus! Amen.

THROUGH IT ALL - Day 4
2:31 PM EDT on Friday, March 23, 2012

Dear Families and Friends,

In the last four hours Elijah has had 2 intense seizures where his lips turn blue; he drools then grits his teeth. Please, we need prayer. After the seizures are over he is very tired and so he sleeps.

We are not sure why he is having so many seizures or why they are so intense. I feel helpless as I watch him sleep, but I'm right by his side. We pray that he is not coming down with some other illness again.

Start praising God because the tempter is trying everything to destroy. Thank You, Lord Jesus, for these seizures right now because I know that Your plan is perfect. We will get through this with You for we are children of God, James 4:7; *"Submit yourselves, then, to God. Resist the devil, and he will flee from you."* (NIV). In Jesus's name, Amen. Praise God! Keep praising everyone. We will keep you posted.

Love and prayers.

Day 4 Continued (9:52PM)

Dear Jesus,

I just want to thank You for today. Thank you, family and friends, for your prayers. I'm coming to you late in the evening and I am so very tired. It has been an extremely challenging day today. Elijah had three intense seizures and I am physically and emotionally drained. I want to thank You Jesus for helping me get through this day and thank You that we can look at this day and realize You, God are in control. We love You and we give honor and praise to You. Tomorrow is a new day and we're looking forward to waking up and being with You as You guide our every step. Good night Jesus! Amen.

THROUGH IT ALL - Day 5
10:33 PM EDT on Saturday, March 24, 2012

Dear Jesus,

Thank You for a very restful sleep last night and thank You for another day to be with You. We are getting prepared for the "New Beginning" that is only two days away. We have not told Elijah yet because for most of his life he has been in and out of hospitals, and the sight of one makes him very upset. Last October, our first visit to Cleveland Clinic, we told him we would stay in a hotel, (this is the Cleveland Clinics guest house connected to the hospital) and then they will take pictures of his head. He was very concerned and said, "No pokes, right?" Our response was...silence. We didn't say a thing, we just looked at each other hoping that it would end at that... and it usually did.

Thank You Lord! We have come to learn with Elijah that you have to be careful with what you say because if we would have hinted about going to the hospital, this would have been a very long week for him, upsetting him, and possibly triggering more seizures. We have seen a pattern that when he is stressed, excited, etc. he is more likely to have them. The plan is to tell Elijah tomorrow, that we are going to Cleveland again. Rick and I will explain the surgery by telling him that they are going to put him to sleep, just like they did for the MRI, and then when he wakes up, our prayer is that those nasty spells will go away. We are not going to use the word "SURGERY"...at all. So, Lord, I just pray that You would prepare Elijah's heart for when we tell him, and that You would share with Rick and I how we can turn this into a less frightening experience for him.

Rick and I know that You Lord, have already prepared the way, so we will not fear. For we are leaning on You God for Your strength and for what You are going to do for Elijah and our family. We thank You for the seizures yesterday because that was Your way of reaffirming in our hearts that this surgery is much needed and Your timing is perfect. We thank You so much for Your constant guidance and direction during this time in our life.

The only thing left to do now is to pack, and we will do that tomorrow. Thank You, Jesus for Rick, driving to meet Manuel (my brother-in-law) half way today to pick up these beautiful candles my sister Sherri made. We are to hand them out and it will serve as a reminder to pray for Elijah on March 29th. These candles have Elijah's picture and when you light the candle, his face lights up. Thank you so much Sherri for all you have done for us as God has used you in a tremendous way. Glory and Honor to God!

Today I made a list of everything that we'll need for our journey. #1 on the list...BIBLE! I like to think the anagram stands for (B)asic (I)nstructions (B)efore (L)eaving (E)arth, but God made a way for us to look at it like this, just for a time... (B)asic (I)nstructions (B)efore (L)eaving (E)pilepsy. That's right. NO MORE EPILEPSY. Thank You, Father for the Bible, Your Word. For without it, we wouldn't be able to see how to live out Your Word in Faith, how You lived on this earth and handled things, and how we have come to know You more intimately and grow in our relationship with You.

We feel so much closer to You when we are in Your Word. We just love meeting with You and spending time with You. You have taught us so much through Your Word. We don't even have to have a meeting place, we can meet right where we are, for You know as well as Rick and I do, that I always get lost. So, Lord, I thank You so much that You have given us a choice to open Your Word and point us in the direction we need to go. Now we understand that when we are not following Your directions, we end up either at a stop sign, a caution sign, or even worse...A DEAD END. That is when we can go to Your Word and know that You are directing us along the right path.

Thank you Lord, for You know us better than we know ourselves, and we know that with You and Your Word we choose not to get lost. We don't even need a GPS, we have YOU. Again, we want to thank You for today. We can't wait to spend another day with You tomorrow as You guide us and direct us as we prepare to leave on Monday. Until then, we'll meet You in Your Word. We love You Jesus! Amen

THROUGH IT ALL - Day 6
8:05 PM EDT on Sunday, March 25, 2012

Dear Jesus,

Thank You, Jesus, for just being You. For the lives' that You have entrusted to us; our boys, Jacob and Elijah; and for showing us Your abundant grace and mercy. Thank you, Jesus, for hearing our prayer and directing us with Your words of comfort as we explain to Elijah about his

"New Beginning." We told him as stated in yesterday's journal and the response was just what we expected "No pokes, right?" Rick and I asked him if he remembered in the past when they put the mask on his face and he fell asleep, and when he woke up he didn't even know that they had given him a poke. That is how we explained it was going to be on Thursday. We assured him that when he woke up those nasty spells were going to be gone. Rick and I both had tears in our eyes when he looked up at us and said, "You mean I'm not going to have any more spells? Whoa Hoo! All right! I'm not going to have any more spells." I then explained to him that he would be able to play out in the sun and run and do everything his friends can do. Can you believe that?

Friends and Family, I wish you could have seen the smile on Elijah's face. It was exactly what we needed to see, and I thank You Lord for another beautiful moment which we were unsure of. I started thinking, oh Father, why didn't I trust You? Why couldn't I have known that this was how it was going to go? Please forgive me, Lord. There are times in our lives when we tend to doubt and then the moment of truth comes, we see it, but we fail to believe it. Thank you for showing us today that example through a child's smile because I visualize that is just how You see us.

When we step out in faith, we know that with Your Word there is no void. I like to picture You slapping Your knee and with a big smile of Your own, say "YES, she finally got it. It's about time."

It's when we learn and act out the real truth that is exactly what You are waiting for. Please help us Father, each day to never miss a moment when You are speaking to us. Please help us to see You in every detail of our lives and live out the moment of truth. We cannot do that on our own. We need You to show us and lean on Your strength, not ours. Mom and Dad Eaton came over and gave us a movie to watch. They told us we need to watch it tonight. The movie was *Soul Surfer*. I was told to listen for a verse in Jeremiah. So, stay tuned till tomorrow to find out the answer. Thank You again Jesus for showing us what true faith is all about through a child's eyes and smile. We love You and we look forward to leaving our home, just for a time, and returning with a child who will begin his "New Beginning." Glory, praise and honor to You, Jesus, Amen.

THROUGH IT ALL - Day 7
11:58 PM EDT on Monday, March 26, 2012

Dear Jesus,

Thank You, Lord, for Your message in Jeremiah 29:11, *"For I know the plans I have for you declares the Lord, plans to prosper you and not harm you, plans to give you hope and a future"* (NIV). This was the verse from the movie we watched last night, *Soul Surfer*. What a great reminder from You Lord. Last night was very difficult for Rick and me; we just held each other and cried. At that moment we both were experiencing the "what ifs?" Please forgive us Father. Last night we really hit rock bottom. Lord, we have been praying for Your will to be done; for You see our hearts. I looked at Rick and he said to me, "Yeah, but Kerri, what if God's will is to take Elijah home with him? I don't think I can go through that again." Then it hit me, "Oh God, we have been through this, we can't go through that again."

Lord you saw our tears. We were just holding each other and we both agreed as comfort was restored, that we had already given Elijah back to you once before God. Father please, this is the most difficult prayer to pray, but both Rick and I have put our hope and trust in You. You know the plans that You have for Elijah, plans to prosper him and not to harm him, plans to give him a hope and a future, but Lord, we pray with every beat of our hearts Your will be done in Elijah's life. Lord, You know us and our deepest desires. You know we have already experienced a loss of our only daughter and we experienced the loss of losing Elijah for two minutes during the code blue, but by Your grace and mercy You gave him back to us. Thank You, Jesus, for we cry out to You and our prayer is that You alone, God receive glory, honor, and praise because You know and already have prepared Elijah's life so we thank You with all our hearts for always being there. You alone are our comforter, our healer, our God.

Tomorrow we have our appointment at 10:25 AM with the pediatrician. This will give us clearance for surgery on Thursday. We thank You Jesus again for your constant guidance and protection as we have arrived safely to our destination.

Now as we go to sleep tonight, may we always remember that You are in control of every situation, so we leave it with You and rest knowing all is well and nothing can compare to what You have already done for us. You carried Your cross - giving honor and glory to Your Father and we thank You for carrying our cross at this moment. We know that You will always be there when we have to carry another cross during this life. We love You Jesus. We can't wait to meet You in Your Word tomorrow. In Jesus' name, Amen.

THROUGH IT ALL - Day 8
9:07 PM EDT on Tuesday, March 27, 2012

Dear Jesus,

God, You have given us so much; Your love, Your faithfulness, Your mercy, Your grace, and the most beautiful gift You have given to us, is Yourself. Not just to us, but to those who have asked You, Jesus to be Lord of their life. To our family and friends, isn't it wonderful to know when we call upon God and we pray to Him, He will listen to us, for when we seek Him, we find Him when we search for Him with all our hearts. Jeremiah 29:12-13 says, *"Then you will call on me and come and pray to me, and I will listen to you. You will seek me and find me when you seek me with all your heart"* (NIV).

We want to say thank you for your continued prayers and support and for sharing in this new beginning with us. Today, we met with Dr. Bingaman for the first time. Elijah had just sat in the chair, listening to every word he was saying, and you could feel the peace and comfort that was in that room knowing we were surrounded by God's presence. Glory to God in the highest. When asked by Dr. Bingaman, "Elijah do you have any questions?" Elijah replied, "Well, um, well, I'm, I'm, a little worried," and Dr. Bingaman replied, "What are you worried about?" Elijah spoke, "I don't want it to hurt." At that moment, Rick and I looked at each other with tears in our eyes. We knew that we were witnessing God's glory being revealed because the Elijah that we know would have ran out of the room screaming. He just sat there calmly with tears in his eyes and said, "Yup and these spells are going to be all gone."

In that moment we took a picture of Elijah and Dr. Bingaman together as a reminder to us to remember God's Word, we walk by faith and not by sight. Thank You, God, for showing us through Elijah, a childlike faith. We are so proud of Elijah. Thank You, God, for Your presence was felt in every appointment we had today. Elijah received a clean bill of health so that we can proceed with the surgery on Thursday. Tomorrow, Elijah will receive an MRI with sedation. He is ready for these seizures to be gone and so are we. Father, God thank You for Your Word, for when You, Lord are so close to us, You become more real than our trials. James 4:8 states, *"Draw near to God" and he will draw near to you" (ESV)*. Thank you Jesus for all You do, for You receive the glory and honor You so deserve. We love You Jesus and we can't wait to meet You in Your Word tomorrow. In Jesus name, Amen.

THROUGH IT ALL - Day 9
10:43 PM EDT on Wednesday, March 28, 2012

Dear Jesus,

Now I lay me down to sleep. I pray the Lord my soul to keep. My God be with me through the night and wake me with the morning light. Thank You, Jesus, for this prayer, for we felt it to be the perfect way to end our night as we prepare for our "New Beginning" tomorrow morning starting at 5:00 am. Since arriving on Monday, we have seen God move in so many ways.

We are so proud of Elijah Lord, thank You so much for showing us through Your strength, with God, anything is possible. Today Elijah was sedated and had his MRI. When we arrived to prepare for the "sleepy medicine" Elijah's spirit was filled with laughter. You can only imagine when the medicine kicked in how much more "goofier" he got. Thank You, Lord, for laughter. Then when the laughter started to wear down, we knew it was time for one of us to go to that bright room with Elijah and watch him as he lay on a hospital bed as they placed the mask on his face. All Elijah could do was call out to me, and all I wanted to do was hold him, but I couldn't. Though he couldn't see me, he knew I was there. The only thing I could do was say to him, "I'm here, Elijah."

Jesus, when we need You, and we're calling out Your name, we can't see You but we know You're there too. We cry out to you Father, and Your presence and comfort is felt immediately. Thank You, Lord Jesus, for today.

Tonight, our parents arrived, along with my sister and her husband Manuel. It was wonderful to see them and to know that their support means so much. Thank you, Mom's and Dad's and Sherri and Manuel for traveling to be with us. Right now, I need to end tonight's journal entry because we need to get up tomorrow at 4:00 a.m. to be ready at 5:30. Lord, we know that tomorrow we will go through the "sleepy time" again, and the wanting to hold him, we'll kiss his cheek and then leave him in Your hands as the doctor's share in this "New Beginning" and You working through their hands healing Elijah. For when Elijah wakes up, the "New Beginning" will have arrived. PRAISE GOD! Glory and honor to You

Lord Jesus. We love You and we'll meet You in Your Word tomorrow. We love You Jesus. In Your Name we pray, Amen.

THROUGH IT ALL - Day 10
Day of Surgery, Thursday, March 29, 2012

9:18 AM
Glory to God, we Praise His name. Surgery began at 8:39 am.

9:56 AM – We were just informed from the nurse that they are beginning the resection now and Elijah is doing great! Thank You Almighty Father. Praise God!

10:41AM - We just received word that Elijah is still in surgery and doing well. Praise the Lord. What a wonderful God we serve for we know He is right in there with him. May God receive the glory and honor He so deserves.

11:43AM – Again, we heard from the nurse; still resecting, which means they are still working on removing parts of the brain. PRAISE GOD! The nurse also says Elijah is doing great! Thank You, Jesus.

1:19PM - Praises to our heavenly Father, glory and honor to You....We were just told that Elijah is almost done and soon we can go be with him in ICU. We are almost ready to begin the "New Beginning." We are going to be taking pictures and the "THROUGH IT ALL" journal will be continuing. God is Good...All the time, even when the circumstances don't seem to be ideal, we have to keep on keeping on with His Word, faith, strength, and perseverance of the Lord. He is always near. Thank You, Jesus Christ. Thank you to all our family and friends who have been praying for Elijah. When we all pray to our Father, we are so close to Him united as ONE. Thank you again.

1:25PM - Talked to the doctor via phone conference. Praise God! Elijah is doing great. No blood transfusion needed. He is moving his hands and legs. He will be in a recovery room in 20 minutes and then we can see him. We are having a "Thank You Jesus!" prayer session.

2:24PM – We're in the ICU with Elijah. He did have one unit of blood according to the nurse, but that is not at all unusual. He wants to turn over but with the IV and catheter they are trying to keep him on his back. He wakes up and goes right back to sleep. He squeezes the nurse's finger when asked. He claimed he couldn't yet he did. He said, "I don't like this," then he said, "Hey" to his Dad.

3:03PM - Elijah said "My head hurts a lot." The nurse said we can give him some morphine. The next 48 hours are still crucial. Then he said, "My stomach hurts" ...of course...he can't eat as he is still coming out of sedation. His throat hurts also because of the tube inserted during surgery.

Dearest Jesus,

All I can say is, You God...to You alone receive all honor all glory all praise to our almighty God. To our family and friends who have been praying for Elijah's surgery; God heard our prayer and He answered.

PRAISE GOD! Today we begin our "New Beginning." The internet seems to be down at the hospital right now. As I was trying to connect, I noticed a lot of blood on Elijah's sheets and calmly went to get the nurse's attention.

Elijah has 3 IV lines and one of the deeper ones came out. Thank you, God, for providing a nurse right away. Please be in prayer because Elijah is running a low-grade temperature which we are told is normal for a brain surgery patient, but we want to watch it carefully.

Tonight, Rick is getting rest and I'm with our brave boy just thanking God for a wonderful day, seeing God move in so many ways. We love you all. Thank You, Jesus. Looks like it's going to be a long night, but with You here, everything is just fine. In Jesus name we pray, Amen.

Written by my twin-sister, Sherri Eaton

Dear Jesus,

Tonight, Rick and Kerri are in the ICU with Elijah, so Kerri has asked me to write the Journal entry tonight. Through it all, we praise You Jesus and we thank You.

We just thank you so much for Your abundant everlasting love and Your presence where healing and wholeness is being restored in Elijah. We praise You Father for bringing Elijah out of surgery safely, back to Rick and Kerri, and thank You for providing Your comfort to them and the family as we patiently waited for the doctor's call. Elijah's surgery was about 5 hours and oh how Your presence, Your love and strength surround us and the feeling of peace we feel with Your closeness. Elijah was so strong and brave. We thank You for Dr. Bingaman and his team, for working through Your hands. As we thank the doctors, we praise and give thanks to You Lord, for You are so good. Your mercy endures forever.

Elijah was in a lot of pain this afternoon. He kept saying "It hurts, it hurts." It just breaks my heart seeing him lying there and looking at Rick and Kerri with tears in their eyes, but Father, I remember Your Word *"Be still and know that I am God"* takes away the pain. The pain medicine couldn't come fast enough for Elijah, and Rick and Kerri too as they were helpless. Elijah was given morphine for the pain and was then able to sleep. We know Jesus, that while Elijah is in ICU, that this is the most critical time, and we should have no fear for we know that You are putting Your arms around Elijah loving and protecting him. God, Rick and Kerri need Your strength as they are very tired. For we know God that when You say You will deliver, You will; when You say You will provide, You will. We praise You Jesus. We shall not fear, for You Lord are our strength.

Rick and Kerri want to thank all their family and friends who continue to provide prayer and support and they love each and every one of you. Family and friends, Elijah is not out of the woods yet. Please continue to pray for strength during these critical stages for his complete healing. Father, we are so grateful that every time we seek You, You can be found. Our soul and spirit seek Your Holy Spirit, for You are our comforter and helper and I thank You for easing Rick, Kerri, Jacob, and the family and friends minds. We always know that we can run to You in time of need and we can feel Your love, comfort, and strength. Jesus we can't wait to be with You in Your Word tomorrow and what marvelous works You have in store for Elijah. We love You Jesus. In Jesus name I pray. Amen.

THROUGH IT ALL - Day 11
8:50 AM EDT on Friday, March 30, 2012

Dear Jesus,

We come to You tonight with adoration and praise, for You God Almighty receive all the honor, all the glory. Father, there are so many things that You have brought comfort to us during this new beginning. We have met so many people that also have something in their life that You are providing strength and guidance. I met an Amish woman today and as we were talking about the trials that we go through in life, she made a statement that really reminded me of Your Word. She said, "You know, I have fallen off the band wagon so many times," and then the Holy Spirit spoke to me and I told her, "no matter whether we fall off the band wagon or not, our God gets us back up and He steers us back onto the path of faith."

Throughout this week, Elijah has shown us how when God's people pray, He listens. Elijah was transferred out of ICU onto the epilepsy floor and he walked for the first time since his surgery. Praise God Almighty! The therapist worked with him today and after they were finished he was so tired. Elijah is still experiencing pain but this is the good pain. Father we know that when we go through pain, sometimes we think that it is difficult for us and what we are going through, but You Lord have shown us through Your Word since the creation and the fall of man, we all will experience pain in some way or another. Father, You have taken this good pain and You have used it to show Your glory and Your strength and draw us closer to You. Thank You, Lord Jesus. We continue to see how amazing You are and how You are working in the lives of people who are suffering. When we arrived on the epilepsy floor of the hospital, we saw so many nurses that had previously been Elijah's care takers. It was wonderful to see them again and we met with hugs.

They remember Elijah because of his personality. There was a moment when we were all in the room and the nurses were getting him situated into bed. Elijah was still groggy from the anesthesia when he looked up at one of his nurses named Rose. He opened his eyes and he said, "I love you." Surprised she asked if he was talking to his mom. Without hesitation he said, "No, I'm talking to you." Our hearts melted. Here he is experiencing all this pain, yet he expressed love, not just to Rose, but to another nurse as well. Thank You, Jesus, for when You died on the cross You showed us love through Your suffering and upon bowing Your head and saying "it is finished," You were telling us, "I love you."

If we are not looking for God in every situation, we may miss something that He is trying to show us. We pour out our hearts to Him, by obeying and praising Him in all situations. We are now resting and Elijah is peacefully asleep. Rick will go back to the hotel and I am going to sleep in the hospital with Elijah. Again Lord, we thank You for bringing such wonderful people into Elijah's life. We also want to thank our family and friends for all they have done to help us prepare for this new beginning.

We can't wait to see what tomorrow brings. We love You Jesus, and we will meet You in Your Word tomorrow. In Jesus name we pray, Amen.

THROUGH IT ALL - Day 12
7:00 AM EDT on Saturday, March 31, 2012

Dear Jesus,

My heart right now is so overjoyed. Something happened today that wouldn't have happened if I had listened to my own reasoning instead of the Lords. What I'm going to do is share with you today's events. Early this morning the surgeons came in and were examining Elijah's head... and then the moment came when they said, "Okay Elijah, we're going to take the wrap off your head." Elijah did not like this at all. He started screaming "Why are you doing this to me, Owww!" This broke our hearts. We stood there and couldn't do anything but comfort him and remind him how strong he is and that we are so proud of him. Elijah is such a strong boy. When the surgeons were finally at the last cover of wrapping Rick and I were not ready to see what we saw. Elijah's incision was in the center of his head all the way around to his right temple. Oh God, help us to deal with this sight. Stillness was present. Thank You, Jesus, for we remembered Your Word says, "Do not fear, for I am with you." God, You are with us. Help us, guide us and show us what we need to do so that Your boy whom You have blessed us with can heal and recover.

The doctors then asked, "How much pain medication are we getting through the IV?" We responded, "He does not have an IV." The look on their faces told both Rick and I that they were amazed that he was tolerating the pain as best he could with NO pain medication. PRAISE GOD!

This began the events today of how God has been leading us to where we are right now as I type this journal entry. God has been so good to Elijah and has shown Rick and me that He is the "ultimate healer." Only the second day after surgery Elijah has been taken out of ICU with no IV for pain. PRAISE THE LORD! Dr. Bingaman, the neurosurgeon came in and confirmed to us that Elijah's MRI looks good. PRAISE THE LORD! He also wanted to inform us that Elijah may spike a fever, and if this were to happen, the fever should not go above 100.8.

Father, we want to thank You for our parents, Mom and Dad Daniels, and Mom and Dad Eaton. They have been here since Wednesday. Mom and Dad Daniels left today and before leaving came in to see Elijah and see how he was doing. They were such a big help, and we thank You Lord for giving us special parents. Elijah has been in so much pain but he is tolerating it very well. PRAISE THE LORD!

Jacob and his friends drove all the way from Marquette Michigan to be with Elijah. They came in Thursday night and left today. God, oh how I thank You for our son Jacob. We have seen how You are working in his life as well as his friend's life and we thank you for hearing our prayers. The greatest gift a parent can do for their child is to pray for them daily; that they become the son/daughter that You have created them to become for they cannot do this by themselves. They need You God for their strength.

As Jacob and his friends came in to say goodbye, Jacob wanted to do something for Elijah, so he got on the internet to see how he could contact Dennis Anderson, Gravedigger from Monster Jam. He was able to talk with someone about how Elijah is such an extreme Monster Jam fan and asked if there was a way for Dennis to lift Elijah's spirit in hopes he could maybe come and visit him. The person on the phone gave Jacob an email address to contact him and so Jacob is patiently waiting to hear from him. We don't know what will come from this but God surely does. We just thank You for how sincere Jacob's heart is toward his little brother Elijah. He loves him so much.

We said our goodbyes which were hard for any parent that has children in college...far away from home, but we're so grateful he was able to be here. God made it possible. PRAISE THE LORD! As we were sitting in Elijah's room, no longer than 3 minutes pass and we see Jacob and his friends re-enter the room. They want to go before You, Lord in prayer and pray with us. This touched us deeply. Thank you, Father, for this moment of being in prayer. There is nothing in this world that can compare to You and going before You, for You will always remain the center of our family. Thank you, Jesus, for that moment.

Jacob and his friends are returning to Adrian tonight and then they will head for Marquette tomorrow morning. Lord, we pray for their protection and safety as they travel back. Thank You Father. Later this afternoon, Sherri and Manuel came in to say their goodbyes and Elijah said "I love you so very much." Thank You, Lord for Sherri and Manuel, for traveling all this way to come be with Elijah. They have done so much for us by helping us prepare for this "New Beginning." Sherri's heart is so tender and I thank her for the love she has for You Father. When I wasn't able to write "THROUGH IT ALL" you filled in the gap and had her write it for us. Thank You, Father, for my sister and for allowing her to be here, even though she is suffering through physical pain herself.

We love going through the events of today and how You have second by second guided each and every step of the day. Being with You we could spend hours and hours of studying Your Word, but we know that is not possible so we cherish this time with You and give our complete self to You.

This journal entry is still being written at 11:45 pm Saturday night and all is well at this moment with Elijah so I want to share with you how God's Glory was seen throughout today, and how awesome our God is. Oh Jesus, praise Your name forever and always, and glory and honor is due to Your name for this new beginning. Thank You for the gift of the Holy Spirit. As we go throughout the day writing this entry, the Holy Spirit is moving me to write what will be included tomorrow. It's all for the honor, and glory of our Father in Heaven, and His precious son, Jesus Christ. We love you.

THROUGH IT ALL - Day 13
1:00 AM EDT on Sunday, April 1, 2012

Dear Jesus,
(Written by Rick's Mom)
Elijah is doing great. He ate, drank, and was up walking twice!
Again, we are thankful Jesus.

1:28PM - Hi Everyone, we had a bit of a setback today. The medical staff wanted Elijah to get up to walk from his bed to the chair which he did okay. Then he had to go to the bathroom and when we were getting him up, his legs gave out on him and he fell down. I caught him just as he went down. Then trying to get him to eat, he threw up. Jesus, we pray that he will regain his strength and will be able to eat. Thank You.

3:49PM - Mom and Dad Eaton arrived and told Rick and I they would stay with Elijah while we went back to the room to get rest. I did not want to leave Elijah, but Rick kept pursuing me to go because I was getting weary without sleep. He was tired and I was tired from the following night of not getting any sleep, but I still did not want to go. Then that still voice inside me said, "You need to go." So, we gathered our stuff and headed for the Cleveland Clinic's guest house. When we got there, I still could not sleep. I hadn't had anytime to just let go and cry out to the Lord so the tears just came flowing. All kinds of tears were flowing: happy, tired, and afraid of the unknown - all of the above. But God in His goodness and mercy rocked both Rick and I to sleep. If I hadn't listened to that still voice, I wouldn't have experienced this wonderful gift God gave to me.

I was sleeping though it didn't feel like it. All the words of God were just being poured out and verses that give comfort and peace were being brought subconsciously to my mind. I can't tell you how amazing this is as I write but this is how the Holy Spirit wanted to reassure me and told me this is to be part of my journal for today. All this was happening while I was sleeping. God said to me, "When you're in God's Word, you are communicating with Him."

Every day you spend time in God's Word and learn about Him, you are gaining spiritual truth that will never leave you if you constantly think about God. In everything you do from waking up in the morning, to going to work, to eating, to breathing. Every single minute we are to ask God for his direction in whatever we are doing. As time goes by and you gain spiritual knowledge, He will reveal to you His Word and what it means. Now, leave the world knowledge out of this. There is nothing in God's Word that is meant for worldly knowledge. This is all spiritual knowledge, and to have spiritual knowledge you have to know Jesus as your personal Savior. To know Jesus as your personal Savior you have to repent of your sins and believe that Jesus died on the cross for you, meaning that he gave up His life by being tortured, physically shedding his blood.

Jesus' accusers hung Him by nailing His hands and feet to the cross. Jesus suffered this terrible physical pain so that our past, present, and future sins can be forgiven. You have to believe that after 3 days He arose again, meaning He came back to life. He showed His nail scarred hands to His disciples so that they could go and share and spread the news that Jesus is alive. He stayed on this earth for 40 days and then He told them He had to leave and where He was going they could not go. Jesus said that they should be happy that He was leaving because when He leaves the Comforter would come. That Comforter is the Holy Spirit. Jesus said He will return but does not know the time, only His Father in Heaven knows. But be ready.

After Jesus was taken up to heaven, He was glorified by His Father and now sits at the right hand of His Father in Heaven. This is the gift you will receive the moment when you accept Jesus Christ as your personal Savior. This gift, when we read God's Word will help us understand what God is trying to teach us. If you do not know Jesus Christ as your personal Savior, then there is no way you can understand the Bible - His holy and perfect Word.

As I continued to sleep, I began to think about Elijah's loss of peripheral vision, which led to my thinking how every human that is born has received five senses...sight, smell, touch, sound, and taste. Then I remembered the Words FAITH, HOPE, TRUST, MERCY, GRACE, FORGIVENESS, LOVE, JOY, PEACE, KINDNESS, and MEEKNESS. All of these Words describe the characteristics of God. Then God told me, "Elijah has lost his peripheral vision but he hasn't lost who I am making him to become." Then He told me we need all or at least some of these 5 senses to experience life. But this does not complete our life. God alone completes our lives, by teaching us through suffering that this is needed to become more and more like Jesus Christ.

Then I heard, "at the moment of." Throughout my life, I have had to bare many crosses. God's timing is perfect. His grace and mercy come at the moment it is needed. He is with you during your trial and suffering, to produce in you perseverance, hope, etc. So, through each trial we are being taught how to overcome suffering by giving God the glory. Without suffering there is no compassion. Then I woke up.

Rick and I went back to the hospital. My parents who had stayed with Elijah reported that he was doing much better; he was up walking around and was finally eating. PRAISE THE LORD! Thank You, Father, for hearing our prayer. In that moment, we were just in awe of God, and how mighty He is. We couldn't even speak. What a wonderful way to end the evening. Rick went back to the guest house and Elijah and I slept peacefully until it was time to wake up and do vitals. If they could just let us sleep for the night. Oh well, Jesus is with us so we have all we need. We love You so much Jesus, and we can't wait to meet You in Your Word tomorrow. In Jesus' name we pray, Amen. My prayer today: Dear Jesus, thank You for another day with You as You go before us guiding the way. Thank You, Lord, for the progress that Elijah has made and the progress that is still to come. Tonight, we had a wonderful surprise. As we were talking, Kim James, a really good friend and sister in Christ, walked into the room. We were so surprised! She drove all this way to see Elijah. I'm not really surprised because that is the kind of wonderful person she is. She would do anything or be there for anyone in a time of need. She prayed with us and then she and I went down to the cafeteria to get something to eat while Rick stayed with Elijah. We had a wonderful time talking about You, Lord and the many things You have been providing. Thank You, Lord, for her loving spirit and desire to serve you daily, and we pray for safety as she travels home. I love you Kim.

Father, we're not sure why Elijah has had a setback, but our trust lies in You. This afternoon we were trying to get him to eat. After only a few tiny bites he threw up not only the food, but his medicine as well. When the doctor arrived, he noticed that Elijah looked very weak, and began to examine him. The day after surgery he was doing great, but then after a few days we noticed he had no control of his left arm. The doctor has ordered a CT scan. Thank You, God for Your spirit of comfort. Elijah was very calm during the CT scan without sedation. Thank You, Lord Jesus. Elijah, we are so proud of you. As we wait for the results of the CT scan Elijah is in bed watching Veggie Tales. We have not yet been able to watch it all the way through without him falling asleep or getting interrupted by a nurse checking his vital signs.

Family and friends, God has heard your prayers. Elijah, as of 9:10 pm is sitting up and again attempting to watch Veggie Tales. We are still waiting for the results but have faith knowing that all will be well, because You, God are in complete control. It may be possible that this set-back is a result of the pain meds. We will wait for the CT SCAN and rest knowing all is well. Thank You, Lord, that we have You to come to in times of need and daily PRAISE. For we PRAISE You God for Your Son Jesus. *"We give thanks to You, O God, we give thanks, For Your name is near; Men declare Your wondrous works"* (Psalm 75:1, NSBA). *"Loving kindness and truth meet together; Righteousness and peace kiss each other. Truth springs forth from the earth, and righteousness looks down from heaven"* (Psalm 85:10-11, NIV). Thank You Lord for Your Word. As we learn, help us to understand it and apply it to our lives giving honor, glory, and praise to You. Thank you, family and friends, for your continued prayers and support. Father, we look forward to another day to live for Your glory and we can't wait to meet You in Your Word tomorrow. We love You Jesus. In Jesus name we pray, Amen.

THROUGH IT ALL - Day 14
11:51 PM EDT on Monday April 2, 2012

Dear Jesus,

We are amazed at how You have healed and restored Elijah's health. Today when the doctors looked at Elijah's head they were happy with the results.

Jesus, what a difference a day makes. We are experiencing the results of coming to You in faith and without doubt. We prayed for Elijah and today he is able to lift his arm and is tolerating the pain without pain medication. Family and friends, we are happy to tell you that Elijah was discharged from the hospital this afternoon and he has been seizure free. Praise the Lord, for God has answered our prayers. We can't thank you enough for all your support. Please still continue to pray for Elijah as he is still not able to use his left hand. He will be getting physical therapy at the University of Michigan Hospital.

God's Word tells us how to approach life. We are to come to every situation with faith; an expectation of His goodness and a desire to do His will. God, all the glory and honor belongs to You, for on Thursday, March 29th, Elijah had come through the brain surgery well and without complications. Then, on Friday he was moved from the ICU to the epileptic floor with no IV for pain medication. Praise the name of the Lord. On Saturday, we saw Elijah starting to get weak. Elijah lost complete control of his left arm and became weak in his legs. Here we were saddened by the loss of losing Elijah's peripheral vision, so thank You God for reminding us to be grateful in all situations. We always let God search our motives, and then we search His will. We waited quietly until He revealed His plan. While waiting quietly, God demonstrated trust like nothing else. It was our way of honoring Him. Right now, we are at the Cleveland Clinic Guesthouse. We will be staying here until Wednesday in case an emergency arises. Thank You again Lord, for showing us that Your love, faith, mercy, goodness, and grace, always endures. As I was writing this and speaking out in Jesus' name, I said aloud "in Jesus name we pray," when Elijah shouted out "Amen!"

We love You Jesus and we can't wait to meet You in Your Word tomorrow. In Jesus name we pray, Amen.

THROUGH IT ALL - Day 15
10:19 PM EDT on Tuesday, April 3, 2012

Dear Jesus,

Today we thank You for another day to wake up not in the hospital, but to be at the Cleveland Clinic guesthouse where Rick, Elijah, and I can all be together. Our thoughts are with Jacob and we wish he could be here so we could all be together as a family, but we know that he is preparing for his exams, ready to end his last semester at Northern. We are so proud of Jacob.

Father, we are so amazed how your power and healing has restored Elijah, and we are filled with thankful hearts. Our "New Beginning" has taught us a few things and one thing that really stirs our spirit is that without this "valley" in our life we would have never come to "begin again." As we have been in the hospital, it is not just us who are waiting for a new beginning. There are other families who we have met whose children are lying in hospital beds, some that are more severe cases than ours. Right now, Father, we lift up to You those families. A three-month-old baby girl named Hannah, who has RSV (Respiratory Syncytial Virus). The doctors don't know how long she will be in the hospital. We pray for Your spirit of healing to cover her body and for Your spirit of comfort for the family.

We met another family who has a two-month-old baby boy named Harrison who is autistic and had open heart surgery. He was next door to Elijah in the ICU unit. We lift up little Harrison and his family to You as well. Father we know You can restore their health and so we pray with Your spirit of faith. Thank You, Father, for allowing us to experience challenges and trials that may come during our lives and thank You Father, for we need not fear, because You are with us every step of the way. You even go before the moment and prepare our hearts for what is to come. Elijah has brought so much joy into our life. People sometimes ask us if it's hard to take care of a child with special needs and my answer to them is "yes, but it's also rewarding." Rick and I have experienced a whole different world, for if Elijah was born with no challenges, we would never have come to know the joy and love that these special children have. This world is full of special children who see so differently than we do. The love they have and show is indescribable. Nothing really bothers them and they face this world, not focusing on their challenges, but with smiles. They have such a genuine and deep caring spirit about them. Thank You, Father, for inviting us into this special world. Yes, it has been challenging, for all parents know with special needs children, but I wouldn't change it for a thing, because each moment in Elijah's life, You have brought us closer to You. Every setback that Elijah has had, we have seen Your glory through and through, even in the time we thought our baby girl was going to be ok. You, Father had other plans and wanted her to be with You. We have seen Your glory revealed, through that moment in our lives and we thank You for showing us that no matter what trials and challenges we face, we face them with Your strength, Your hope, and Your love.

Today has been a very restful day. Elijah has been doing his exercises and talking more and more. We are so proud of him. He is able to move his left arm, but his hand and fingers still remain unmovable. Father, we pray that You would heal his left hand. Elijah is eating McDonalds and watching Veggie Tales. Lord, thank You for everything You have provided for us, and we thank You for our family and friends who are continuing to lift Elijah up in prayer to You. Father, thank You for always being by our side and teaching us that You walk with us, You talk with us, and You dwell within us through it all. Thank you, Lord, Jesus, for we can't wait to meet You in Your Word tomorrow. In Jesus name we pray, Amen.

THROUGH IT ALL - Day 16
12:00 AM EDT on Wednesday, April 4, 2012

Dear Jesus,

How can we thank You enough? Elijah woke up this morning and is able to use his left arm and hand. We stand in awe of how God has restored Elijah's health. He is finally seizure free! Thank You, Father God.

We are so thankful for who You are. God, we love You so much, not only for healing Elijah, but for Your presence that is so powerful and the strength and love that You have shown us throughout our life. As we arrive home we see that you have given us a beautiful gift. When we left for Cleveland Clinic on Monday, March 26th, both Rick and I looked at each other as we watched Elijah walk out the door and saying, "Well here we come God. May we come back home with a new child that can live a normal life."

As we returned home today we were not only coming home with Elijah being healed and seizure free, we came home to Your beautiful creation of flowers and colors from my favorite all time hobby...gardening. All of our flowers were in bloom which we thought we would have missed. But God in Your grace and mercy, You saved this for us. We gratefully smiled and said, "We're home."

God, Thank You so much for Your creation. You knew what would bring a smile to our faces as we were greeted by our little blue bird out by Jaelynn's memorial tree. You knew the perfect timing of today as we arrived home with Elijah. When Jaelynn passed away, we came home with empty arms. It was so very difficult. Thank You, God for our arrival home today, for we did not come into our home with empty arms. We had Elijah with us.

As we look around we can see that God is present, even in His creation we see His goodness. Elijah is doing very well. Today as he was watching Veggie Tales, he stopped and said, "Mom, write this in the journal. God made us very special and He loves us very much." How precious! I love you Elijah, and I am so glad we are home and are seizure free. Lord, we look forward to waking up tomorrow morning in our own beds and looking outside at Your beautiful creation. We enjoy it so very much. Who knows maybe we'll see a bluebird again. I hope so. We love You and can't wait to meet You in Your Word tomorrow. In Jesus' name we pray, Amen.

Written by my twin sister, Sherri Eaton

Kerri and Rick, oh how God amazes me with His Word and with your faith. As I read your journal, I feel the Holy Spirit warming my heart. I am amazed at the precious moments you are experiencing as a family and what God has in store for your "New Beginning." Elijah is such a beautiful child of God and I am so glad that God chose you and Rick to be his parents; who would love him and bring such joy to his life. As I read your journal tonight, God whispered to me, "now is the time," the perfect time to share a poem I had stashed away in my drawer for the right time. It is a poem written by Erma Bombeck. This special poem is entitled, "Ode to Moms," but in my opinion it should be named "Ode to Moms and Dads."

This very special and heartfelt poem is written to explain how God chooses the parents of handicapped children. Some might feel that this is a punishment when actually the opposite is true. Those who are blessed with these special children are special themselves and are instead to be envied.

Thank You, dear Jesus, for Rick and Kerri. I love You Jesus.

I love you all so much.

Love Sherri

THROUGH IT ALL - Day 17
9:26 PM EDT on Thursday, April 5, 2012

Dear Jesus,

Thank You for our second day home. We are recovering well and our hearts are overflowing with joy as we remember that every day when we wake up is a moment to give to You. Thank You Lord as you continue to prepare, guide and teach us that all we need to think about is today, not tomorrow or the next; just today. Every breath we breathe is a breath of praise to You God for Your Love. Thank You, Father, for when we woke up this morning, the swelling that was noticed on

Elijah's right temple last night, has gone down. Help us Lord not to get anxious for nothing but to trust Your Word and believe that You, Lord have everything under control.

We are thankful that we have You all the time. It's not just a one-time thing. We can meet You anywhere, anyplace, anytime. Even when I wake in the middle of the night, I fall asleep again knowing that You are watching me and I visualize You rocking me to sleep. This helps so much. Thank You, Jesus. Today was a little chilly outside, but the colors of the flowers and new growth is very beautiful. I showed Elijah and he too was able to enjoy their beauty. Thank You, Lord, for not taking all of Elijah's vision. We are so proud of Elijah, for he is dealing with losing his peripheral vision well. Elijah can only see what's in front of him and nothing from the left side, but he has not complained or said anything about it. He does bump into doors sometimes. His all-time favorite thing to do is to play with his DS Nintendo video game system, though he is not able to do this yet, his spirits are good. He just says, "One day, I'll be able to play." That's all he says. Oh, if I could have more of a child-like faith. Yes, I fall, and I doubt. God, please forgive me. Show me more and more each day how to grow and become more like You, not doubting, but to live my life for You by obeying Your Word.

You tell me not to worry, so I should not worry. Why is that so hard to obey? You tell me, yet I do the opposite. During this "New Beginning," I am learning not to take my eyes off of You God. If my eyes start to wander, I will close them and pray, Lord set my eyes on You, and believe that my prayer has been heard. I then start praising Your name God. I will keep my eyes constantly on You.

Thank You for Elijah and how he has shown me so much through what he is going through. He always has a smile on his face and is always singing, especially when Veggie Tales is on. In yesterday's journal we wrote about how God shows us through his creation (a crested bluebird) that He is always near. Rick went out to the bluebird house where the mamma and papa bird had created a nest; leaving two tiny blue eggs. This is a perfect example that we should not worry because God even provides for the birds of the air. How much more will He provide for us. Thank You, Father, God.

This afternoon, Pastor Darren came over and brought Elijah a Star Wars book and cards that the kids from church had made for him. As I was reading them to him he started to cry. Oh, how this broke our heart; he misses them so much. Thank you, Pastor Darren, for visiting and sharing God's Word with us. Thank You, God, for all those children who brought joy to Elijah's heart. It meant so much to us.

The next four weeks are critical. Elijah will be getting the stitches out in a couple of weeks and we must be careful in protecting his head while it continues to heal. Thank you, friends and family, for your continued support and prayers. We will not worry, for our eyes are on You God. Thank You, Father, for another day to see You, and know You more intimately for You are our God, Father, Redeemer, and Friend. We can't wait for what You have for us tomorrow, and can't wait to meet You in Your Word. We love You Jesus. In Jesus name we pray, Amen.

THROUGH IT ALL - Day 18
9:51 PM EDT on Friday, April 6, 2012

Dear Jesus,

Today we thank You for our third day home. It has been so nice to be in our own surroundings where Elijah can rest and heal. Elijah is doing the best he can after his surgery. The pain has been manageable with Tylenol and he needs to keep his head elevated so the pressure does not cause fluid build-up. He has done very well. Thank You again Jesus. PRAISES TO YOUR NAME.

Though we are home, my heart goes out to those families that we met while in the hospital and we continue to pray for them. Thank You, Father, for continually watching over us. My mom stopped over today to bring Elijah a couple of DVD's and asked if she could take him to Subway. He was so excited. When they returned, I asked mom if she could watch Elijah so I could mow the grass. While I was mowing, I was purposely looking at the tops of the evergreen trees. I remember hearing this amazing truth a couple years ago. If you look at the top of the evergreen trees the week before or the week after Easter you'll see new growth shaped like a cross. As I looked at our evergreens it looked like new growth was just starting. I will continue to watch for those crosses atop my trees. Anyone who has evergreens, keep looking for those little crosses. It's a moment of God showing His Glory. I just love it!

When I finished the lawn, Mom told me that during their lunch outing God had placed them at the right place at the right time. While Elijah was standing in line at Subway, a little girl and her mother were looking at Elijah as if they knew him. The mother asked if he was Elijah, and Elijah answered yes. She said "We have been praying for you." Elijah got a big smile on his face and enthusiastically said, "Thank You." Isn't that amazing! Thank you, Father, for all the people who are praying for Elijah, even those we don't know. This evening mom Daniels brought tacos over for us. They were so good. Thank you, Mom's, for you have been such a great help throughout our "New Beginning." We love you so very much.

Every day we see God's hand in our lives and how He provided all of us, His children, with a new beginning. For on this day, Good Friday, You gave up Your life for all Your children by choosing the cross, becoming the perfect substitute for our sins and giving us Your righteousness. Thank You Lord for changing our nature for when we give our lives to You we become a new person. "We are given a "New Beginning" and are reconciled to You FOREVER. Thank You for today Jesus and Thank You that three days later you arose from the grave. We just can't wait to celebrate the day of resurrection of our Lord, Jesus Christ. HE'S ALIVE! You have made this all possible for all Your children. What we have to do is accept You Jesus as our Lord and Savior, believing by faith You died on the cross and rose again on the third day!

He is preparing us for His return and His free gift of eternal life; to live forever with Jesus. He takes us just as we are, and He creates in us a new spirit, a new beginning. A change in oneself will occur and the desire to obey Jesus will be overflowing because when we love Him we will obey Him. (John 14:15) Thank You, Father, for our family's third day home. We are finally SEIZURE FREE! You have made this all possible and we give You alone all the GLORY, HONOR AND

PRAISE. I Love You Jesus and I can't wait to meet You in Your Word tomorrow. In Jesus name we pray, Amen.

THROUGH IT ALL - Day 19 & 20
8:40 PM EDT on Saturday & Sunday, April 7 & 8, 2012

Dear Jesus,

Thank You, Father, for these last few days. Your Word is life, and Your gospel is for all who have eyes to see and ears to hear. You are ALIVE! Today, yesterday, and forever! Thank You that Elijah has been doing so well. How amazing God, for You are always near, holding us close. We thank You for the healing. Elijah said today, "My head doesn't hurt, but it sure does itch!" All we could say to that is PRAISE GOD! Elijah just gave us a big smile.

Father, we ask for Your protection as we drive to Cleveland tomorrow to have Elijah's stitches removed. Rick is unable to go with me so my friend Stephanie will be joining Elijah and me. Father, I want to thank You so much for my husband Rick, bless his heart. He booked us a room about 20 minutes away from the hospital as the area near the hospital is in a dangerous area of town. We will still be close to the hospital but in a much safer location. Elijah is so happy now that we told him about the hotel and he is less anxious about getting his stitches out. Thank You again God for Rick that he worked it out for us, because deep down I know You were speaking to Him. You are amazing.

Elijah has been tired, but that is expected. Thank You, Lord, for all our family and friends who continue to lift up Elijah and our family. We have felt Your presence surrounding us and we are so blessed by You and the friends and family You have brought into our lives. There are no words to express the gratefulness we have for each and every one of them.

Easter Sunday was wonderful. Saturday, we spent the day at Mom and Dad Daniels and all the grandkids and Uncles and Aunts were there. Elijah hadn't seen his cousins in a while so he wanted to be "down at the farm." Saturday evening his head was a bit swollen. He hadn't done much, he mostly sat on the couch and was on his feet very little, but he was exhausted; too much excitement at Grandma's. Sunday, we went for dinner and the food was wonderful. Mom and Dad Eaton came over in the evening to see Elijah. We had a great time with them.

We really wanted to be with our church family on Easter and celebrate with them, but Elijah needed rest so we are looking forward to being with our church family next Sunday. Father, please protect Elijah's head, and also that we have no set-backs, for we know that the next 4-weeks are critical. The time has passed so quickly since the surgery. We thank You Lord, that when we look to You in every situation, every prayer lifted up, we await Your direction, and listen vigilantly for Your calling.

I can't stop thinking of Hannah, the little baby girl whose parents we met in the hospital. We pray for her parents, and Your spirit of complete healing upon her little body Lord. God, You have a very special way of showing us through people what You can do to make a scary situation in a hospital for a child, less scary, and more comfortable. I loved how, as Rick and I walked into the ICU, in front of the pediatric doors and on top of the soap dispensers were animal puppets. Some had dogs; others had bunnies, cats, and tigers. Elijah's puppet was a lamb. Out of all the units in ICU, there were 2 lambs. Later, talking to Hannah's mother I learned that the other lamb was just outside her room. Wow, Lord, You certainly are watching over us, Your sheep. God, thank you for Your Word for I am reminded in John 10:7, Jesus told us that *"I am the gate for the sheep"* (NIV). In John 10:9 Your Word says, *"I am the gate. Whoever enters through me will be saved. He will come in and go out, and find pasture"* (NIV). In John 10:11 Your Word says, *"I am the good shepherd. The good Shepherd lays down His life for His sheep"* (NIV). John 10:14 tells us, *"I am the good shepherd. I know my sheep and my sheep know me"* (NIV). And finally, in John 10:15 we read, *"Just as the Father knows me and I know the Father, and I lay down my life for the sheep."*

Father this is why we celebrate Good Friday for You laid down Your life for us...We are Your sheep. In John verse 10:16 Your Word says, *"I have other sheep that are not of this sheep pen. I must bring them also. They too will listen to my voice and there shall be one flock and one shepherd"* (NIV). Thank you, Father, for helping me understand this verse John 10:17, *"The reason my Father loves me is that I lay down my life - only to take it up again"* (NIV).

To be raised from the grave. EASTER SUNDAY, Jesus You're ALIVE! Just like a shepherd, His sheep that He takes care of will only follow His voice when called. Jesus, You are our "Good Shepherd," and we are Your sheep. The other sheep You are talking about in verse 16 are those that are not of Your sheep pen, and have not given their lives to You, but You know them by name and are waiting for them to hear Your voice. He's calling You to join His sheep. Will You listen or choose to stay out of the shepherds pen?

Father I pray with all my heart that those who do not know You as their personal Savior, that they will hear You calling them and enter into an intimate personal relationship with You. I pray that they come to know You with all their heart, with all their soul, and with all their mind. We have seen how You have restored and continue to restore Elijah's health and today, April 8th, 2012, Elijah is SEIZURE FREE! PRAISE GOD! We were expected to still be in the hospital but were discharged after only 4 1/2 days. Thank You so much. We give You all glory, honor, hearts of PRAISE and THANKFULNESS for what You have provided for us on the cross. For You gave Your life for us so that our past, present, and future sins are forgiven and that three days later, you arose from the dead and now LIVE! God's Word is for everyone. The gospel John 3:16 *"For God so loved the world that He gave His One and only Son that whosoever believes in Him shall not perish but have Eternal life"* (NIV). (G) Gospel (O) Only (S) Son (P) Perish (E) Eternal (L) Life. Thank You, Father, for calling us Your sheep.

Each day Lord, guide us and teach us to become more and more like You, as we graze in Your pasture, as we read Your Word and apply it to our lives. For we PRAISE YOU for the ETERNAL LIFE we are NOW living TODAY because we, Your sheep, accepted You as our Shepherd, Lord, and Savior. We love You Jesus, and we will meet You in Your Word tomorrow, In Jesus name we pray, Amen.

THROUGH IT ALL - Day 21
12:18 AM EDT on Monday, April 9, 2012

Written by my twin-sister, Sherri Eaton.

Oh, how wonderful today has been for Elijah, Kerri and Rick. Thank You Jesus for You know what is going to happen before we do, as we put all our trust in You. Today, Kerri, Elijah and Stephanie drove down to Cleveland Clinic to have Elijah's stitches removed. We praise You, Jesus, for protecting them during their travel for there was never any doubting. *"The Lord, He is the one who goes before you. He will be with you, He will not leave you, nor forsake you, do not fear nor be dismayed"* (Deuteronomy 31:8, ESV). We thank You so much Jesus, for Rick being able to return to work and giving him and Stephanie's husband comfort and a peace of mind, that they are in good hands; God's hands. Thank You that they were able to make it safely to Cleveland.

Elijah had his stitches removed at 3:00 pm today and everything went well. Thank You, Jesus. We love You so much and we Praise YOU!!!! Elijah has a low-grade temp so the doctors wanted to draw blood to make sure there was no infection. Tonight, Kerri, Elijah and Stephanie are safe back at the hotel watching, *"Happy Feet 2."* Kerri will be writing Day 22 tomorrow. We Praise You God, for You always give the best present to all of us.... YOU. Thank You for our family and friends who have been continually praying for Elijah's healing. As we all close our eyes and go to sleep tonight, we thank You Father, for always providing Your love, trust, mercy, glory, hope, grace, and forgiveness to us all. Whatever you are going through, and it is a safe assumption to say that we are always going through something; it is not to negatively affect God's provision. God is above all circumstances, and He is greater than your sin. Bring it all to Him, your sin, and your trials; you're everything. Bind yourself to the things that really matter and the One who can govern and protect them; Jesus Christ. And rest. Be at peace and be well. We love You Jesus and we can't wait to meet You in Your Word tomorrow. In Jesus name we pray, Amen.

THROUGH IT ALL - Day 22
8:46 PM EDT on Friday, April 13, 2012

HAPPY BIRTHDAY ELIJAH!
Jesus made it possible for us to be home on your 12th birthday. Praise His name, forevermore.

THROUGH IT ALL - Day 23
4:10 PM EDT on Saturday, April 14, 2012

Dear Jesus,

Ascribe to the Lord, you heavenly beings, ascribe to the Lord glory and strength. Ascribe to the Lord the glory due his name worship the Lord in the splendor of his holiness"(Psalm 29:1-2, NIV).

Father, thank You for your constant guiding and direction as we stand before You, for having a God that we can turn to day or night and seek Your protection. I can see that You have been surrounding Elijah with Your comfort, courage, and strength because he has handled this very difficult time in his life with a smile. Even though the pain is there and he feels that something is different, he doesn't cry, or get upset. He is content. I know this because when he touches his head, and he looks at me smiling he says "I love you Mom." Oh, that just melts my heart and I look to God at that very moment and say "Oh Jesus, thank You." For through a child You are showing us that no matter what we are going through, physical, emotional, or spiritual pain, You are looking into our eyes and saying "I love You."

This last week was full of surprises, and we thank You God for each one because if we would have done things the way we wanted to, it wouldn't have worked out the way You planned, so I thank You for Your complete and constant hand that was upon us this week.

When we arrived home on Wednesday April 4th, we had been healing and doing wonderfully. Thank You, Father, for the spirit of healing upon Elijah's head. The next best thing to happen was getting the stitches taken out. The doctors told us upon discharge that we could get the stitches out in either our own ER department or at his pediatrician's office. I was very surprised considering this was a major surgery and especially with the brain involved, so as we prayed and asked God for direction. We were directed to Elijah's neurologist from Toledo, Dr. Nagel. His nurse called us and said that Dr. Nagel advised us to go back to Cleveland Clinic to have the stiches removed. Thank you again Lord, for the patience You provided in us. If we would have listened to our own direction we would have taken the easy way and stayed here in town to get the stitches out. For what we discovered when we arrived in Cleveland Clinic, would be more surprises yet to come.

Rick couldn't make the trip because he had to work, but he really wanted to be there. Again, Stephanie made arrangements with her family so she could go with me so I wouldn't have to go alone. I am so thankful God that she was able to go because I wouldn't have been able to do this physically myself. Monday, April 9th was the big day to leave for Cleveland Clinic to get the stitches out. Elijah was so excited! When we woke up he was doing great. I went to pick up Stephanie and headed for McDonalds because Elijah was hungry. As we continued our journey Elijah kept saying "I don't feel good, Mom, my stomach, I don't feel good." Suddenly Elijah started throwing up. We were only 5 minutes from the house so we returned home so that we could get him cleaned up. Again, we started for the Cleveland Clinic. Once we were back on the road Elijah was feeling much better and was fine the rest of the way there.

When we arrived, Elijah was not nervous at all. In fact, he was very excited. Ann the neurosurgeon nurse took us back and sat him down to take his temperature. His temperature was slightly elevated at 99.1 which was not much of a concern but she did ask us to monitor it. As they started to take out the stitches, God, Your Word came to mind from Job 1:21, *The Lord gave and the Lord has taken away; may the name of the Lord be praised"* (NIV). This reminded me of when Jaelynn passed away. A few days after her passing, I wrote this verse in her journal I was keeping throughout my pregnancy, and even though it's not the same as what we were going through that day, this was Your way of telling us "I know everything about Elijah, what he is going to go through. I knew he would have brain surgery, I knew he would be alright. I knew that he would have a spike in his temp, I knew that he is going to have 37 stitches taken out, but these stitches had to be there because this is how I was going to work in Elijah's life by removing the parts in his brain that were not working so that he can begin to have a better quality of life. So, Yes, I gave Elijah's these stitches, but watch I will now take them away." PRAISE GOD! Thank You, Lord, for that special moment with You. I could now turn to Elijah and say "Let's get those stitches out!" I then noticed the smile on his face. He came through it wonderfully and all thanks to our God. What a WOW moment!

After the stitches were removed, Ann the nurse felt that it was necessary to get blood drawn to make sure his white blood count was normal, and that the levels from the meds were where they were supposed to be. His throwing up earlier could have been a sign of infection. I am so proud of you Elijah. You did a great job getting your blood drawn. After these appointments we had made arrangements to stay in Cleveland for one day because Elijah loves to stay in hotels (he calls them Mo-Hotels), I think because he heard us say hotels and motels and didn't understand, so to this day it's mo-hotels. Elijah, you make us laugh.

After going to bed I woke up at around 1:00 am to check on Elijah. He felt warm to the touch and his heart rate was very fast. I took his temp and it was 101.7. Ann had told us that if his temp rose to over 100.4 he needed to go to the ER immediately as this could indicate an infection. We all quickly headed for Cleveland Clinic, 20 miles away. When we arrived at the ER in Cleveland, they were able to get him in right away. Praise GOD! The results from the blood work showed that his white blood count was high which means infection. The doctor wanted to do a CT scan to make sure everything was okay. The results were positive, he was fine. Another PRAISE! Around 7:00 am they admitted him to monitor his temperature. If it continued to increase, he would have to have a spinal tap. Fortunately Elijah's temperature stabilized. I remember praying to You God, please let us be home for Elijah's birthday. On Thursday morning we had three teams of specialists on Elijah's case, the neurosurgeons team, the pediatric team, and the neurologist team. All were very nice. Thank You, Lord, for the gifts You have given to these men and women to help those in physical need.

Later midafternoon one of the pediatric doctors came in to ask Elijah if he was ready to go home. All I could do was cry. I was so happy, and relieved because Stephanie was tired, I was tired and I know Elijah was tired. We just wanted to be home with our families, and God thank You for making that happen. We arrived home Thursday evening at 9:00 pm and Rick met us at the door. Elijah couldn't get his seatbelt off fast enough. As I looked at them hugging each other all I could do was cry. It wasn't sad tears; it was happy tears because I knew that our "New Beginning" was starting on Elijah's Birthday, April 13th, 2012. We celebrated Elijah's birthday and he loved every minute of it. Just as Jaelynn's new beginning started when she went home to be with her Heavenly Father, Elijah's new beginning was starting over with a better quality of life here on earth. What a blessing God provided for us. Our daughter's "New Beginning" in Heaven, and our son's "New Beginning" on earth.

We will all have a "New Beginning" when Jesus Christ our Savior comes back to bring us all home to our permanent home...Our eternal new Heaven. Thank You, Jesus, for all You have shown us through our "New Beginning." Our new beginning has just begun. The doctors predict that total recovery will take 1-2 years, so our journal is continuing because all of this is for the GLORY OF GOD! God is always present. We always have to be searching, seeking, and waiting patiently for Him to take us THROUGH IT ALL! Thank You, Lord

Jesus, for we can't wait to meet You in Your Word tomorrow. WE LOVE YOU! In Jesus name we pray, Amen.

THROUGH IT ALL - Day 24
9:34 PM EDT on Monday, April 16, 2012

Dear Jesus,

Thank You for another day filled with healing and seeing Your hand upon Elijah. Father, we are so thankful to our families and friends who are lifting up Elijah and our family in prayer.

Today, Elijah is very tired, which the doctors did say is to be expected. Thank You, Lord, that on Sunday we were able to go to church. Seeing our church family and being in Your presence was exactly what we needed. Thank You so much for pastor Darren and the passion and adoration he has for You and Your Word. Elijah was so excited to be back, and see his good friend Elliott. It was a wonderful day.

When Elijah is up and on his feet he seems to be more tired than usual but again, we know this is a normal part of his recovery. Father, we thank You so much as Elijah continues to be SEIZURE FREE! His incision is healing beautifully. Tomorrow we have an appointment with his pediatrician, and we thank You that You have brought us this far. Father God, I know I can come to You just as I am; and I am tired. It makes me so happy when I know deep within my soul I can come to You as a little child comes running to their parent. Every moment, in good times and in hard times, for I know that each day as I release my problems, fears, doubts and discouragements upon You, a little of myself dies because I'm not relying on myself, I'm relying and giving all of my life to You Father. Thank you for reminding me of Your promise.

Today I had a chance to go out and clean up my flower beds. I love to garden, and this was the perfect time because Elijah was sleeping. When I looked at my flower bed, all I wanted to do was come back inside because I knew with all those weeds; it was going to take a while. But if I had chosen to go back inside, I wouldn't have received the message You wanted to tell me through the weeds. I have bright red tulips but the weeds were covering them up. So, as I'm pulling the weeds I am noticing how beautiful and bright the red tulips are appearing and how beautifully they stand out. Father God, guide us each day as we live in this world. Open our eyes to the weeds (sins) that need to be removed from our lives so that You, can stand out, for You are beautiful and perfect in every way. Thank You, Lord, for another day to give glory and honor to Your name. Tomorrow is a new day and another beautiful moment to meet You in Your Word. In Jesus name we pray, Amen.

We're back!
Day 25 – Tuesday, April 24, 2012; (9:35 pm)

Dear Jesus,

Thank You for the days we have been able to be home. No hospitals or emergency visits, just recovery and rest. Father, we thank You for each and every one of our family and friends who continue to pray for us. Elijah continues to be seizure free and his head is healing well. There are times when he says "Mom, I have a headache," and I say to that "Well, Okay Elijah, we'll get you some Tylenol." To you that might sound funny, but to us it is amazing because Elijah has never been able to tell us he has a headache. Since he was six months old, pain has been a part of his life and he had learned to accept it. But PRAISE GOD! Because God knew that He (God) would deliver Elijah from those frightening seizures. Thank You, God, for beginning our "New Beginning" on Elijah's birthday. We were discharged from the hospital... a second time; the day before his birthday, and what a celebration. Elijah gets tired easily, and this is acceptable. We have five weeks of complete healing yet to go. Father, this "New Beginning" has been really different for us. Not that I'm complaining or anything, but since we've been home, it's like arriving home with a new baby. Elijah is completely seizure free, and all his life we've lived with facing these seizures and now it's like "Okay, what do we do now?" I told Rick I think I have post-partum depression because all I do is feel like crying and I'm really tired. Thank You, Lord for Your Word, because we can go to it and read Your instruction as to how we can turn our temporary moments of sorrow into teaching moments with You. As I start to read in Matthew 5, I'm being drawn to the Beatitudes. Father, thank You for being so alive when I'm in Your Word. As I sit here and write, it's amazing what the Holy Spirit is leading me to write about through our "New Beginning." God thank You; for You will show me through my sorrow what Your Word says and how I am to apply it to my life. Lord, take us to the Sermon on the Mount. Family and Friends, as we continue to update you on Elijah, we're going to start our "New Beginning" teaching Elijah how God teaches us in the Sermon on the Mount. If you would like to follow along and share with us what God is placing on your heart, we would love to hear from you. We can learn together as God leads us and directs us, as we call upon His name and apply His Word to our lives. We are so excited as to where, what, when, why, and how the Holy Spirit will lead us always giving Glory and Honor to God. This "New Beginning" has been very exciting for us because God continues to surprise us every day. I love how You, God, always show us how powerful You are to create every living thing our eyes can see. We now have 6 baby crested blue bird eggs and soon they will hatch. We love You Lord, and we're looking forward to learning about the Sermon on the Mount as we meet You in Your Word; tomorrow. In Jesus name we pray, Amen.

A Prayer of Salvation

Dear Friend,

Jesus loves you, and I care so deeply for you and where you will spend Eternity. This book was not only written to share my story, it was written for you; to share God's message of salvation. He's calling you to take that leap of faith. All you have to do is surrender to Jesus and make Him Lord of your life.

If you are ready to take that life changing step, pray this prayer:

"Father, I love You and I believe You died on the cross for the forgiveness of my sins.

Please forgive me of my sins and help me to begin again with strong roots.

I cannot do this on my own, so lead me as I walk with faith, hope, and Your love.

In Jesus name I pray, Amen

Welcome to the family of God!